T0344840

# RE-CONSTRUCTING

## CROSS-BORDER E-COMMERCE

# RE-CONSTRUCTING CROSS-BORDER E-COMMERCE

## THE GLOBALIZATION PRACTICES OF SMALL AND MEDIUM-SIZED ENTERPRISES

—

## LI XINXIN & PENG XIAOLING

Translated by Daniel McRyan

上海交通大學出版社
SHANGHAI JIAO TONG UNIVERSITY PRESS

naturalogic

Re-constructing Cross-border E-commerce:
The Globalization Practices of Small and Medium-sized Enterprises

Li Xinxin and Peng Xiaoling
Translated by Daniel McRyan

Copyright © Shanghai Jiao Tong University Press

Published by NATURALOGIC PUBLISHING INC., under an exclusive license with Shanghai Jiao Tong University Press.

First English Edition 2021
ISBN: 978-1-4878-0481-7

www.naturalogicpublishers.com

19-1235 Johnson St. Coquitlam, BC, Canada V3B 7E2

# PROLOGUE

Historically, it is the states that propelled the first globalization. And the states' will is embodied whether in the Great Geographical Discovery or in the state companies represented by the East India Company. The second globalization is driven by multinational corporations. Over 6,000 multinational corporations dominated 80% of global trade. Yet, the third at present is pushed forward by small and medium-sized enterprises (hereinafter referred to as SMEs) and the young generation. A more widely beneficial and sustainable globalization has been achieved as they took great advantage of the infrastructure and business model of the digital economy.

In most countries, SMEs are the main body in the business structure. There are nearly 12 million micro and small enterprises and 44 million individual businesses in China. In the digital economy, the development of cross-border e-commerce platforms led to a lower cost and threshold of international trade. Therefore, significant changes have taken place in trade subject, trade form, business models, and organization mode.

Via cross-border e-commerce platform, even micro and small enterprises are able to establish contact with customers and suppliers in other countries, which opens a window of opportunities for the development of SMEs. And e-commerce and related service ecology also empower them with the competence to rival large enterprises. The last generation of globalization was steered by large enterprises, but the steering wheel of that in the era of digital economy falls into the hands of SMEs.

Alibaba Group is committed to paving an easy path to every business operation through the provision of convenience for micro, small, and medium-sized enterprises and consumers around the globe. From an e-commerce platform, widely beneficial finance, intelligent logistics to big data, cloud computing, and cross-border e-commerce services, Alibaba Group enables micro, small, and medium-sized enterprises and consumers to 'buy, sell, pay, transport, and travel globally' in the search of more innovative growth by providing a new business infrastructure of the digital era.

In March 2016, Jack Ma, Chairman of the Board of Directors of Alibaba Group, proposed Electronic World Trade Platform (eWTP), appealing to help micro, small, and medium-sized enterprises to thrive, reducing trade and investment barriers, and formulating new rules of trade in compliance with the trend of digital economic development. In September 2016, the eWTP initiative, as a core policy proposal of G20 business exercises (B20), was written into the communiqué of the G20 Leaders' Hangzhou summit.

Over the past two years, eWTP has received positive acceptance and active support within the international community. In March 2017, the first eHub (a digital hub) outside China was launched in Malaysia. In May that year, interconnection was officially activated between the two digital hubs of eWTP, the Malaysia digital free trade zone and the Hangzhou cross border e-commerce comprehensive pilot zone. In July 2018, Belgium announced its accession to the eWTP, thus launching the first European eHub in Liege, Belgium.

Meanwhile, eWTP, the World Trade Organization (WTO), and the World Economic Forum (WEF) embarked on the collaboration on Enabling E-commerce.

Cross border e-commerce is setting up a free, open, general, and inclusive global trade platform. On this platform, hundreds of millions of consumers can 'buy globally' while micro, small, and medium-sized micro enterprises can 'sell globally.' It is a true realization of global connectivity and global linkage. It can be predicted that cross-border e-commerce will connect the world and evolve into the prevailing form of global trade in the future.

It is hoped that this book can export the new paradigm of globalization practice of China's SMEs, provide reference for more of them to go beyond the border, inspire them to adopt new business models to locate new growth spots of business development, and truly become practitioners of 'buy and sell globally.'

*Gao Hongbing*
*President of the Ali Research Institute*

# EDITORIAL

Since the beginning of the 21st century, the commercial Internet is the fruit of the co-action between the new technology colony represented by the Internet, the Internet of things, big data, cloud computing, and artificial intelligence, and the new business model represented by e-commerce. Today, the development of the global digital economy has unprecedentedly changed our way of life. Whether it is the number of Internet users or smart phone holders behind these figures, the data proves that technology, commerce, and the economy are undergoing drastic changes. Simultaneously, the changes are restructuring cross-border e-commerce and propelling the transformation and upgrade of traditional industries. It is exactly the original intention of this book to outline the new business environment more clearly and locate the changing direction of new trade, so as to help more SMEs succeed in going global.

At present, cross-border e-commerce has formed a business collaboration ecosystem that can accommodate the participation of various roles. A more profound perception of the essential problems and business laws will contribute to a better understanding of the development of the cross-border e-commerce industry and the Internet, and to the identification of a future direction. Among the major participants of cross-border e-commerce: SMEs, a large number of "shapers" have emerged in the times of transformation. As thought leaders and innovators, they are redefining the rules of the new era with new patterns of thinking, new business models, and surging passion.

It took a year for this book to go from planning, research, and writing to publication. The editors visited a great many SMEs that have adopted B2B cross-border e-commerce as the primary business model and that have successfully been transformed. They were deeply involved in the activities of various small and medium sized entrepreneurs to explore the core competitiveness of different business models. Consequently, in the combination with typical cases, a collection of case studies has been composed that concentrates on the exploration of cross-border e-commerce business outlines and the analysis of SMEs' successful models towards globalization.

At the same time, I would like to thank Alibaba's partners for their strong support during the publication of this book, for selflessly sharing the latest research results and market research data on global trade, and for their advice at critical nodes; I would like to thank the small and medium sized business owners who received the interviews, for being pioneers in the transformation of the times and willing to share their successful experiences without reservation, so that more readers can have the chance to have a comprehensive and diversified understanding of cross-border trade.

While the trend of trade wars remains unclear, global trade is inevitable. The external market environment is complex. For every small and medium sized enterprise owner, only a correct aim at new opportunities can realize the reconstruction of industry, organization, and values. Finally, we sincerely invite every reader to join us to realize your new mode of going beyond the border!

# TABLE OF CONTENTS

## PART I

### China's New Foreign Trade: Alibaba and the Globalization Practices of SMEs

## PART II

### Chinese Suppliers

# PART I

# CHINA'S NEW FOREIGN TRADE

## Alibaba and the Globalization Practices of SMEs

# CHAPTER I

# The New Chapter of Future Globalization with Inclusive Sharing

O N NOVEMBER 29, 2017, Jack Ma expounded at the World Convention of Zhejiang Merchants held in Hangzhou: "To run an enterprise, a leader must set up, take advantage of, and follow the trends. It is difficult to set up a trend, but it's important to follow and take advantage of it." Today's technological revolution is a trend, China's "One Belt One Road" initiative is one, the mode of global industrial chain cooperation is another, and the way of global cooperation and development in the future will also be one.

"Today and today's China are the best for business." It is the question that every entrepreneur and every young person desire to ponder and crack how to grasp the pulse of the times to realize the resonance of individual transformation and technology trend, of enterprise development and national strategy, and of business profits and social values.

\* \* \*

## Has globalization really ceased?

### *The Failed Globalization of Multinational Corporations*

For some past time, the voice of anti-globalization was everywhere.

On June 24, 2016, the United Kingdom decided to exit the EU after the referendum. And European Union suffered the first blow of downsizing. And the chaos continued. In France, Holland, Italy, Sweden, and Denmark, the political parties that favor anti-globalization have won public support. For example, the Italian left-wing political party that actively advocated a withdrawal from the Eurozone earned a high support rate.

President Trump is more of an anti-globalization advocate. In January 2017, the first presidential order he signed after taking office was to announce the withdrawal from the TPP (Trans-Pacific Partnership Agreement) negotiations. Over the past year, under the "US Priority" policy, US trade economic protectionism has gone through continuous consolidation, and the restrictive measures have expanded from manufacturing and agriculture to digital economy and innovation-intensive industries.

So, what led to the occurrence of the political events against globalization, and how come the public support? What are the reasons and logic that lie behind?

For a long time, developed countries as the European countries and the United States have been the leading forces of globalization, and multinational corporations have been the main drive for the rapid development of the last round of globalization. Targeted at profit maximization, multinational corporations transfer investment to developing countries with lower labor cost and lower requirements for ecological environment and social security. While globalization has gained them more profits, they also lead to the imbalance of interest distribution, which eventually has given rise to anti-globalization.

One is the imbalance of distribution among different countries. Due to the division of labor in the global industrial chain and value chain, labor-intensive manufacturing industry is mainly located in developing countries under the global production and outsourcing system. As a result, the corresponding unemployment rate in the manufacturing sector of developed countries in Europe and the United States has surged. These unemployed workers have become the main anti-globalization groups.

The other is the imbalance of distribution within the country. In the process of economic globalization, the distribution of interests of different countries is unequal and imbalanced. Low-income groups and disadvantaged groups profit less while large enterprises and social elites benefit more. In *Capital in the Twenty-First Century*, Thomas Piketty, a French economist, made a comparative analysis based on a large number of historical data and concluded that the return of capital far exceeded the income of labor, and the "scissors gap" would grow increasingly larger. The "winners" who benefited from globalization ignored the demands of low-income groups, intensified the exposure of social contradictions, and led to the prevalence of Western populism.

In fact, anti-globalization is more than a political trend of thought. It is actually taking place in reality.

The UK is a large trading partner of China, only second to Germany in the EU. Many Chinese companies have set up branches or headquarters in the UK. On March 16, 2017, the UK officially launched the Brexit procedures. And Chinese enterprises may no longer be able to enjoy the European market tax exemption, or even have to consider whether there is the necessity to move the European headquarters out of the UK.

The United States is China's largest trading partner in the world. And US priority indicates that the American interest comes first. As a Chinese enterprise, when doing business with the United States, one may come across a very good investment opportunity to merge and acquire an American enterprise. Even if it is a win-win situation, it may also be turned down because of "US priority." The survey data of Thomson Reuters shows that as of November 2017, the mergers and acquisitions scale of Chinese capital in the United States in 2017 decreased from $60.36 billion in the same period of 2016 to $13.88 billion, a decrease of nearly 80%.

At the beginning of 2018, the Sino-US trade war was brutal. On January 2, 2018, the United States rejected Ant Financial Services Group's acquisition of MoneyGram on the grounds of national security. In addition to investment, better and newer products could have been sold to the United States at the trade level, but now it is no longer plausible because of "U.S. priority." On January 9, 2018, AT&T, a U.S. carrier partner, abruptly aborted the plan to sell Huawei mobile phones in the United States at the last minute during Huawei mobile phones' first entry into the United States. On March 22, 2018, U.S. President Trump signed a presidential memorandum at the White House to impose tariffs on Chinese products exported to the United States. The imposed tariffs will be on $60 billion of goods imported from China and Chinese enterprises' investment in the United States will be restricted.

Therefore, it is noticed that, against the trend of globalization, international trade is more difficult to conduct. It is not that the market is bad, but that the resistance is greater. In the foreseeable future, the game between globalization and anti-globalization will further develop in depth vertically in economy and trade, investment, science, and technology.

The sea of the world economy has both calm tides and raging waves. Is today's thought of anti-globalization trend a torrent of trends or a wave of adjustment? Has globalization really ceased?

The description of China's President Xi Jinping in the 2017 World Economic Forum gives the answer: "The sea of the world economy, whether you like it or not, is there, inevitable. It is impossible and against the trend of history to cut off the flow of capital, of technology, of products, of industries, and of people in the economies of all countries and have the sea of the world economy downsize to an isolated small lake and river."

For the trade war waged by the United States since 2018, President Xi Jinping demonstrated the attitude China holds at the Hainan Asia Bo'ao Forum on April 10: "In the light of a comprehensive assessment of the general trend of world development, economic globalization is an irreversible trend of the times. And it is based on this assessment that I stressed in the report of the 19th National Congress of the Communist Party of China that China would adhere to the basic state policy of opening up to the outside world and to opening up the country for better construction. I want to make it clear to you that China's open door will not be shut tight. Instead, it will only open wider and wider."

**CASE STUDIES**  In the Sino US Trade War, has the anti-globalization trend been established?

On March 22, 2018, U.S. President Donald J. Trump of signed a presidential memorandum at the White House to impose tariffs on Chinese products exported to the United States. It proposed to impose tariffs on US$60 billion of goods imported from China, and to restrict Chinese enterprises' investment in the United States. The Sino-US trade war broke out, stirring up widespread concern in the market.

On April 3, the Office of the United States Trade Representative released a list, involving about US$50 billion worth of goods imported from China each year, of goods to be taxed according to the results of Investigation 301. Later, China's Ministry of Commerce announced in the afternoon of April 4 that China had decided to impose a 25% tariff on 106 goods originating in the United States, with an import amount of about US$50 billion. The news immediately triggered a sharp reaction in the U.S. market. Soybean, pork, beef, and other futures prices plummeted. The futures of the three major stock indexes all fell by more than

1.5%. Boeing dropped by more than 5%, Ford over 2%, and General Motors more than 3%. The market reacted strongly. Obviously, the trade war will have a negative impact on the import and export of both China and the United States.

In terms of imports, on March 23, China's Ministry of Commerce issued a list of products subject to suspension and concession in response to the 232 measures for the import of steel and aluminum products from the United States and solicited public opinions. It is planned to impose tariffs on some products imported from the United States. China has terminated tax reduction for seven categories and 128 tax products, including fresh fruits, dried fruits, nuts, wine, American ginseng, seamless steel pipes, pork, and waste aluminum. Accordingly, for the cross-border e-commerce engaged in the import of fresh food and nuts, the product costs will increase due to the increase of tariffs, and the market will inevitably be impacted. In terms of exports, according to the memorandum signed by U.S. President Trump, the Investigation 301 will impose high tariffs on China's multi-field imports and restrict China's high-tech investment in the United States. This impact will make it more difficult for China's electronic equipment, mechanical equipment, clothing, and metal products to be exported to the U.S. market.

What measures should China's cross-border e-commerce enterprises take in the face of a fierce trade war?

First, additional value and competitiveness of products should be strengthened. In the trade war, the United States listed the issue of intellectual property infringement as an important factor against China. In the future, enterprise competitiveness will always be built on more importance attached to intellectual property protection, and enhancement of product innovation and brand promotion brought by design, creativity, and technology whether from the perspective of consumers' consumption trends or product competitiveness.

Second, diversified markets should be expanded. With the development of China's "Belt and Road Initiative" and constant opening up of the Chinese market, markets in Europe and other developed regions, as well as developing countries such as India and Brazil, will continue to create opportunities. A diversified market strategy will reduce the policy risk brought by a single country.

Is the anti-globalization trend really established?

The answer is negative. Data shows in the past decade, China's export dependence has been declining, and the proportion of exports to GDP has decreased from 35.4% in 2006 to 18.5% in 2017; the proportion of trade surplus to GDP has fallen from 7.5% in 2007 to 3.5% in 2017. The amount of US$60 billion is merely equivalent to 2.64% of China's exports in 2017. The impact on scale is therefore not fatal.

For a long time, Sino-US economic trade has been regarded as the cornerstone of bilateral relations. The logic behind lies in the complementarity of Sino US economic trade: China provides cheap household goods that the United States would rather not produce; a large number of Chinese-contracted factories reduces the manufacturing costs of American enterprises; China purchases a great many American agricultural products, and aircraft. However, China gradually poses a threat to the profit of the US in the trade as it continues to catch up in science and technology, and finance and large-scale equipment manufacturing in the process of an industrial upgrade. For example, the C919 aircraft casts a great impact on Boeing. Therefore, the United States announced to impose tariffs on US$60 billion of Chinese goods to punish China for infringement of intellectual property rights. The internal reason is that China will find itself at rivalry against the United States more often in the process of industrial transformation.

So why does China stand in a firm posture in this trade war? On April 6, the spokesman of the Ministry of Commerce gave the answer: "This is a fight between unilateralism and multilateralism, a fight between protectionism and free trade." China is more resolutely opening up and integrating into the global trading system, and there will be more defenders of globalization in the ocean of the world economy. In April 10, 2018, President Xi Jinping solemnly declared in the opening speech of the Hainan Asia Bo'ao Forum that China would massively relax market access, create more attractive investment environment, strengthen intellectual property protection, and take the initiative to expand imports. "We will implement these major measures of opening up as soon as possible. The sooner the better. We strive to ensure that the results of opening up benefit Chinese enterprises and Chinese people, and the enterprises and people around the world as soon as possible."

### *The Digital Economy Assembles the Global Chain*

President Xi Jinping clearly explained at the first stage conference of the 24th APEC In-formal Leadership Conference: "Economic globalization has entered a stage of adjustment. Naturally, there are voices of doubt and hesitation. It should be noted that economic globalization is in line with the requirements of productivity development and the interests of all parties. And this is the trend that none can resist."

Why is economic globalization the general trend?

Globalization has formed a community of common destiny between countries for years. The world is where no country is absolutely isolated but somewhat connected. The economy between countries stays inextricably linked, and the degree of interdependence is constantly strengthened in both developed and emerging countries. Take Alibaba.com as an example. Some post-90s-born clients who received company start-up service on the platform have the company located in Qianhai, Shenzhen, the products designed in Israel, quality control performed in Germany, customer service based in the UK, and production workshops constructed in Cambodia and Vietnam. And the annual sales reach over RMB 100 million.

Globalization is characterized by the change from globalized production to globalized lifestyle. People's endogenous demand for good quality and low price remains unchanged. On the one hand, the trend of anti-globalization is surging. On the other hand, one has to admit that everyone is enjoying the low-cost goods and diversified services that come with the free trade: airplanes, cars, smartphones, and the Internet we use. The outcomes of economic globalization are not made solely in either one country or one place. For the demand of high-quality yet low-cost products and services, service outsourcing gains popularity, cross-border tourism blooms, and overseas shopping thrives. All factors of production, including all kinds of people, resources, and funds flow freely around the world. People's adaptation to the lifestyle of globalization allows both economic and social problems to transcend national boundaries thus requiring coordinated responses from all countries.

The Internet has accelerated the assembly of the global chain. And the digital economy has made it impossible for the global division of labor to reverse. In the past decade, the penetration rate of the global Internet has climbed from 21.7% to 48.8%, while the growth rate of Internet penetration in developing countries is double that of developed countries. The rapid development of infrastructure has bred the digital economy, which makes global cooperation an inevitable choice. Digital technologies in the digital economy, such as big data, cloud computing, and artificial intelligence, are in wide application. Relying on the "Digital Nerve" platform, the update cycle of products and services accelerates. Therefore, speed has become a key competitive factor. Enterprises must, at the fastest speed, grasp the latest market demand trends and hot spots, transform them into products and complete production and manufacturing, and adjust marketing strategies and implement them. The pressure of speed pushes enterprises to achieve a global division of labor in a cooperative manner. On the other hand, the technological revolution has greatly reduced the infor-mation cost of communication, making it possible to cooperate extensively and at a low cost. The rapid development of the digital economy gives rise to another side of the world outside the "offline world" in the past – "online world." The flow and sharing of data enable the business process to cross the enterprise boundary and weave a new resource network, ecological network, and value network. In the near future, companies will become intangible, but the market and business will cover the entire world.

"Historically, economic globalization is the objective requirement of the development of social productivity and the inevitable outcome of scientific and technological advancement. It is neither the creation of people nor countries. It has provided a strong impetus for world economic growth, and promoted the flow of goods and capital, the progress of science and technology and civilization, and interpersonal communications of all countries."[1] Globalization is no longer a dispensable option, but a powerful engine of world economic growth and social progress of every country.

Jack Ma stated in the 2018 Davos Forum: "Should people still use mobile phones in 30 years, they can make global purchase. For example, if you want to buy something from Kenya, one click does the trick; if you want to buy something from Norway, click it. Global purchase, global sales, global payment, global delivery, global travel, all can be done on mobile phones. A passport may no longer be needed. This is bound to happen in 10 years. This is a message. Let's seize the opportunity. And when you do that, the next Alibaba is yours."

What is the volume of the digital economy?

- As of June 2017, the total number of Internet users in the world reached 3.89 billion, with a penetration rate of 51.7%. Among them, China's netizens reached

---

1. Cited from the keynote speech *Together We Shoulder the Duty of Times, Together We Promote Global Development* delivered by President Xi Jinping at the opening ceremony of the 2017 Annual Session of The World Economic Forum.

751 million, ranking first in the world, and the number of global mobile users reached 7.72 billion.

- 22% of global GDP is closely related to the digital economy covering skills and capital, and China's digital economy accounts for 30% of GDP.
- Among the top 100 multinational enterprises in the world, 19 are high-tech or telecom enterprises, whose total market value accounts for 26% of the global economy.
- China is the world's largest e-commerce market, accounting for 40% of global transactions.
- China's mobile payment also takes the lead in the global industry, with transaction volume 11 times that of the United States.
- The world Internet development index shows the United States ranks first with 57.66 points, and China the second with 41.8 points.[1]
- In the next five years, private online consumption will grow at an annual rate of 21%, and online shopping will contribute to 42% of the growth of private consumption.[2]
- 39% of online retail sales in China is new consumption, and in third tier cities and below, the percentage goes up to 57%.[3]
- In 2035, the overall scale of China's digital economy will grow close to US$16 trillion, the penetration rate of digital economy will be 48%, and the total employment capacity will reach 415 million. Among them, the employment scale of the Alibaba economy will exceed 100 million.[4]

## *Spark of Cross-border E-commerce*

The international political pattern constantly changes and there are repeated ripples in in-ternational economic activities, but the cross-border trade at the level

---

1. All data in articles one-six is obtained from the blue book World Internet Development Report 2017 and China Internet Development Report 2017, released by the Fourth World Internet Conference.
2. Source: Report on China's Consumption Trend: Three Emerging Forces Leading the New Consumption Economy, a cooperative report by the Boston Consulting Group and the Ali Research Institute.
3. Source: *China's Digital Transformation: The Impact of the Internet on Productivity and Growth*, published by the McKinsey Global Institute.
4. Source: *Research Report Towards the Future of 2035: 400 Million Digital Economic Employment*, released by the Boston Consulting Group.

of SMEs and consumers has become increasingly frequent. Gradually, they are taking the responsibility of globalization instead of multinational corporations.

Globally, the global online retail trade volume increased from US$860 billion to US$1.920 trillion from 2011 to 2016, with an average annual growth rate of 17.4% according to the survey of eMarketer, a third-party data organization. In 2016, the global e-commerce market size exceeded US$25 trillion, becoming a bright spot and a new growth point of the world economy. The scale of online retail transactions in the United States reached US$371 billion, an increase of 8.5% year on year, accounting for 8% of the total retail sales in the country. It is estimated that by 2020, the global online retail transaction volume will exceed US$4 trillion, accounting for 14.6% of the total global retail volume, a huge increase compared with 7.4% in 2016.

Thanks to this, the cross-border e-commerce market will welcome a leapfrog development. Nielsen's report shows that propelled by the Internet, it will maintain 300% growth in the next five years, while Accenture's research predicts that it will reach US $994 billion in 2020.

For China, China's cross-border e-commerce is growing despite the slowdown in global trade growth, and the penetration rate of e-commerce in import and export trade continues to go up.

According to the statistics of the Ministry of Commerce, the annual growth rate of China's total foreign trade was merely 0.3% from 2012 to 2016, while China's cross-border e-commerce transactions maintained an annual growth rate of more than 30% from 2011 to 2016, from RMB 1.7 trillion to RMB 6.7 trillion, a nearly 5 times increase. Cross border e-commerce has become a crucial driving force for China's foreign trade growth, accounting for 27.53% of the total import and export in 2016, an increase from 8.6% in 2012.

In 2017, the scale of cross-border e-commerce transactions in China reached RMB 7.5 trillion, up 25% year on year. It is estimated that it will amount up to RMB 13 trillion in 2020, with a compound annual growth rate of 22% during 2015–2020. The penetration rate of e-commerce in China's import and export trade continues to ascend. In 2017, cross-border e-commerce transactions accounted for 27% of China's total import and export. The percentage is expected to rise to 35% by 2020.

So, why did cross-border e-commerce emerge as a new force and gradually became rebellious in anti-globalization? Why did the tiny spark of China's cross-border e-commerce ignite the world?

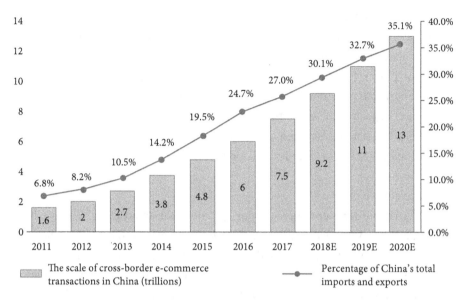

The scale of cross-border e-commerce transactions in China (trillions)

Percentage of China's total imports and exports

**Figure 1.1** Transaction volume of cross border e-commerce in China and gross value of imports and exports

*Source: Ministry of Commerce, General Administration of Customs, Iresearch.cn, analy-sys.cn, Ali Research Institute; Analysis of Ali Research Institute.*

This would not have come true without the four drives: technological advancement, consumption upgrading, industrial support, and credit assurance.

- *Technological advancement*

The great progress of science and technology has opened the good timing for cross-border e-commerce now that the popularization and development of Internet and intelligent terminals have constructed a good infrastructure for it. Consumers or dealers can make a purchase at any fragmented time. The improvement of payment system and logistics system promotes the optimization of a transaction. Without bugs, concern in breach of contract, and endless waiting, the satisfaction of a transaction has been massively improved; cloud computing and big data encourage consumer's demand to promote large-scale flexible production, "produce before purchase" becomes "demand before production," which grossly improves the personalization and satisfaction of the procurement. All these have paved the road for the development of cross-border e-commerce.

- *Consumption upgrading*

China has a huge market. In 2020, there will be nearly 200 million middle-class and above households in China. Consumption upgrading provides an inexhaustible source of power for the development of cross-border e-commerce. Therefore, China's enormous consumer market, which is able to not only absorb the domestic production capacity, but also attracts broad international attention, becomes the weight of trade balance between China and other countries, thus creating a good opportunity for SMEs to "buy and sell globally."

- *Industrial support*

China's cross-border e-commerce exports account for about 80%. Why is China able to go beyond the sea? The answer is that China has the most comprehensive manufacturing industry in the world, forming a huge development advantage. All types of Chinese goods, from machinery to home furnishings, from 3C digital products to fashion consumption, go abroad. According to the research findings of Dr. Wang Jian, professor of the School of International Economics and Trade of the University of Foreign Economics and Trade, there are around 5 million SMEs in China's foreign trade, accounting for about 60% of the total volume. If they can make full use of e-commerce and big data to better understand the overseas market and the demand trend and illuminate the direction for production, China will become evolve from a manufacturing strength into a manufacturing power.

- *Credit assurance*

Cross border e-commerce takes place between strangers, so communication security is the priority. As goods are shipped across the sea and funds transferred across the continent, no business can happen without credit assurance. The cross-border e-commerce trading platform represented by the Alibaba international station has effectively reduced the transaction impediment of cross-border e-commerce and promoted the continuous development and simplification of transactions by forming a positive cycle of emphasizing credit to promote trades. Take the Sandra family business in Alibaba international station as an example. A few years ago, many African clients would make a field trip to China before placing orders. Only when they saw the factories for real were they finally assured to engage in the trade. However, with their growing trust in Alibaba international station and the platform's provision of credit assurance services to solve trust risks for buyers, an increasing number of clients have completed transactions through

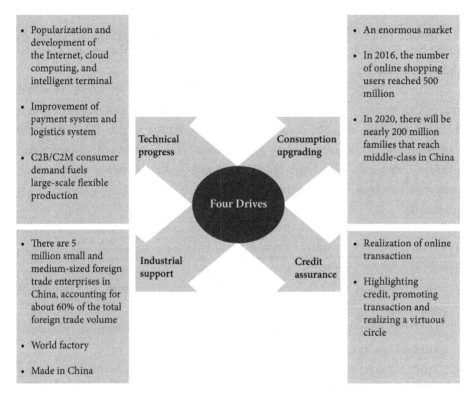

**Figure 1.2** Four drives for the rapid growth of China's cross-border E-commerce

online communication. Basically, an e-commerce platform can replace the offline visits.

Is the core value of cross-border e-commerce a simple provision of a new platform for enterprises? Obviously not. The core value is to provide directive guidance and transformative opportunities for the upgrading of national manufacturing industry and service industry via the clear understanding of consumer demand and the foresight in market changes.

To realize the value, data is the key. Cross border e-commerce enables every enterprise to directly face the needs of consumers and receive feedback from them and quickly grasp the development and change of the market to predict its future trend. Consequently, this shall propel the transformation and upgrading of manufacturing and product supply as a whole, reduce the intermediate links and inventory, and enable enterprises to obtain greater profit space.

Cross border e-commerce relies on the platform to create a complete industrial chain. It includes a complete data chain from manufacturing to export, and then to the final overseas consumers. It also includes a complete industrial chain of marketing, logistics, design, and production carried out by the enterprises with the help of data.

Cross border e-commerce has set up a free, open, general, and inclusive global trade platform, on which hundreds of millions of consumers can purchase goods around the world, and SMEs can sell goods around the world. This is the true realization of global connectivity and linkage. The cross-border e-commerce platform represented by Alibaba international station benefits SMEs of all countries with inclusive and win-win global trade by reconstructing conventional trade links.

## An overview of China's cross-border e-commerce data

- The proportion of China's cross-border e-commerce exports and imports is about 4:1.
- In 2012, exports accounted for 88.57% of China's cross-border e-commerce transactions and imports 11.43%.
- In 2016, the exports volume was RMB 5.5 trillion (the same below), accounting for 82.1%; the import volume was RMB 1.2 trillion, accounting for 17.9%.
- In 2017, the export was RMB 15.33 trillion, up by 10.8%; the import RMB 12.46 trillion, up by 18.7%; the trade surplus was RMB 2.87 trillion, down by 14.2%. In 2017, the overall transaction scale of cross-border e-commerce (including retail and B2B) reached RMB 7.6 trillion. In 2018, it is expected to climb to RMB 9 trillion.[1]
- The proportion of B2B and B2C of cross-border e-commerce in China is about 9:1
- In 2012, B2B accounted for 96.2% and B2C only accounted for 3.8% of cross-border e-commerce.
- In 2016, the trading volume of B2B was RMB, 5.94 trillion accounting for 88.7%; that of B2C was RMB 0.76 trillion, accounting for 11.3%.
- In the first half of 2017, the trading volume of B2B was RMB 3.15 trillion, accounting for 87.4%; that of B2C was RMB 0.45 trillion, accounting for 12.6%.
- In 2017, the volume of B2B transactions exceeded RMB seven trillion, and B2C

---

1. Source: *2017–2018 China cross border e-commerce market research report* released by Aimei Consulting.

surpassed RMB one trillion for the first time, and the proportion increased to about 12.5%.

*   *   *

## Future globalization

The future globalization is the one that we are experiencing today. It is a globalization in which SMEs and consumers are deeply involved and in which the imbalance of interests is broken and benefits are shared.

### Global cooperation in the digital age

In the future, the cross-border consumption of individuals and small entities will gradually push globalization to a new climax.

In the era of cross-border e-commerce, the improvement of the cross-border transaction infrastructure will make it easier and cheaper for individuals to directly participate in cross-border consumption, which will contribute to the development of an inclusive sharing globalization. It includes:

(1) Global innovation cooperation that is centered on consumer demand. The cross border e-commerce platform makes it more convenient and efficient for consumers to access commodity information. The development of social media promotes information sharing among consumers and global cooperation centered on consumer demand. Through the cross-border trading platform, a seller can connect with global consumers, understand their needs, and conduct direct transactions; a consumer can effectively grasp the manufacturer and market information, and communicate with consumers in other regions via social platforms to share products, manufacturer information, and personal experiences, and enhance their say to inspire enterprise on micro innovation and achieve customization and innovation of products and services without borders.

(2) Global service cooperation that is driven by technical support. The advancement of machine translation can also assist both parties to overcome language barriers. The cross-border development of the third-party payment

platform reduces the cost, simplifies the process, and improves the timeliness of individual cross-border payments, and motivates other payment service providers to improve their cross-border payment services. The deepening of the logistics system can meet the requirements of fragmented transactions and flexible transportation and delivery in a small batch at a lower cost.

(3) Global industrial chain cooperation that is based on data sharing. By 2020, the relevant data of billions of cross-border transactions of nearly one billion consumers every year will be generated on the cross-border e-commerce platform, which is a valuable asset on the platform that can considerably benefit many parties. These data will help global enterprises to understand the characteristics and needs of consumers, service providers to judge the market more accurately, and even governments to achieve more accurate policymaking and decision-making, as well as tax revenue realization. As a result, the overall cooperation of the global industrial chain shall be formed.

The new globalization model will propel the more comprehensive and in-depth development of commodity economy, and constantly meet the higher quality and individual needs of consumers in terms of supply, so as to guide the global economy to a fairer and inclusive track. Globalization based on Internet and cross-border e-commerce will bring:

(1) More transparent information. Based on the Internet and information technology, consumers understand the products, order placing and purchasing, goods shipment around the world with logistics, etc. via the Internet. A large number of information flow generated in these links will alleviate the information asymmetry between enterprises and consumers in the market, and illuminate the path for enterprises to identify customers, update products, and innovate ideas. Cross border e-commerce not only meets the needs of consumers, but also encourages their pursuit of different aspects of the commodities. While leading consumption, cross-border e-commerce also broadens the access to information for domestic enterprises in the industry, which contributes to less information asymmetry between the two parties.

(2) Fairer competition. The cross-border e-commerce channel unifies the domestic and international markets. Through the e-commerce platform, safer, richer, and higher quality products are provided to consumers at home and

abroad, and more choices are made available at lower prices. This is to have the enterprises of a certain product and industry compete with each other in the world and may the fittest survive in fiercer competition.

(3) A more prosperous market. On the one hand, a more transparent and fair market environment will fertilize the healthy competition of enterprises; they have to constantly make adjustments in differentiation, personalization, and quality to adapt to the forever-changing market, which will be conducive to better meet the needs of consumers, the future development of the industry, and the requirements of supply reform. On the other hand, the enhancement of productivity brought by the Internet will reduce a large number of traditional positions. In the new economy, new forms of employment continue to emerge. Cross border e-commerce will create more job opportunities for countries by promoting platform employment and creating jobs in the service sector.

### Opportunities of globalization for SMEs

In the future, globalization will change the division of the global industrial chain led by multinational companies. SMEs and other micro entities will gradually take over, becoming the center of the next stage of globalization through the development of cross-border e-commerce.

Under the influence of the Internet, the changes of people's production and lifestyles allow the products provided by SMEs to be flexibly adjusted and easily accepted by the terminal market.

Great changes have taken place in people's shopping ideas and styles. For example, people are increasingly used to and prefer electronic transactions online, and the form of trade is gradually flattened; the convenience of the mobile Internet enables people to use their fragmented time to conduct online transactions anytime and anywhere; the order amount shrinks large to small, the time cycle reduces from long to short, and the transaction mode develops from mass production sale to fragmentation, customization, and personalization.

The trade characteristics of flattening, fragmentation, customization, and personalization have minimized the advantages that large enterprises and trading companies once had to none. On the contrary, the flexibility of SMEs can faster adapt to the changing needs and make corresponding adjustments in time for the changes. Thanks to an accurate grasp of the market demand, SMEs make production in a more flexible fashion. As a result, it is easy for the products to be accepted by the terminal market, and they gradually become the new force for further development in the foreign trade share.

The inclusive sharing of infrastructure greatly reduces the transformation cost of SMEs, and then lowers the bar for them to participate in globalization.

In the past, traditional information technology (IT) products, epitomized by servers, storage, and software, suffered from high procurement and maintenance costs. Today, in the era of big data, the on-demand services represented by cloud computing enable individuals and various enterprises to obtain necessary computing, storage, and network resources at a low cost without acquiring expensive hardware, software products, and equipment. Therefore, the technical bar is greatly lowered, making cloud computing an inclusive technology.

Cloud computing has ended the monopoly of large enterprises in computing power and gradually has become the basis of an inclusive economy. SMEs have acquired the professional ability that was only available to large enterprises before. The inclusive sharing of infrastructure greatly reduces the transformation cost of SMEs, and then lowers the bar for them to participate in globalization.

Under the trend of open innovation, small-and medium-sized, enterprise-styled micro innovation will be more recognized and transformed into a huge driving force for social and economic development.

Back then, when it came to enterprise innovation, people used to think more about the R&D centers of large enterprises such as Microsoft and IBM. With sufficient capital and talent, they rely on internal resources for closed and self-circulating innovation, and constantly improve the competitiveness of the enterprises. The cost of such innovation is too high for SMEs to afford.

Nowadays, "side job," "slash life," and "passive income" are what the younger generation pursue and is more discussed in daily conversation. For self-realization and more financial freedom, a growing number of young people are trying to realize their dreams with micro wisdom. Individuals or SMEs can quickly locate suitable business models such as funding, technical support, outsourcing, teaming, consulting, or strategic alliances form through the Internet while turning innovative ideas into real products and profits faster and better.

Every innovation point of SMEs will cast a very considerable impact on the mature market. Many micro innovations that were considered insignificant gained more benefit and stronger competitiveness for faster speed and lower cost.

Consequently, they were paid more attention to and turned into a huge driving force for social and economic development.

Eyepatch's founder, Michael Sorrentino, is a media practitioner with more than a decade of experience. A report on a hacker's invasion of a school's computer system encouraged him to start his own business. He designed a mobile phone case that can block the front and rear cameras at the same time. When one wants to take a photo, a soft slide of the cover will expose the camera to be used. In addition to maintaining the camera of the phone, it also helps users avoid the potential risk of privacy leak.

With a simple sketch on paper, Michael found an ideal Chinese supplier on Alibaba, which not only offered prototype 3D modeling, but also design modification suggestions. Later, in the form of crowdfunding, the privacy protection phone case was mass produced in a few weeks. Soon, it was reported by BuzzFeed, a popular news aggregation website for young people, and The Verge, a well-known technology website, and was officially endorsed by Apple.

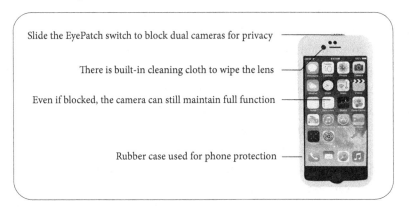

**Figure 1.3** Eyepatch's privacy protection phone case

---

1. Source: Inspirational Stories on CES, Alibaba international station helps the young generation in the United States to grasp the opportunity [EB / OL], (2018-01-12). Http://www.ce.cn/xwzx/gnsz/gdxw/201801/12/t20180112_27707773.shtml

### *A new chapter of inclusive sharing*

Today, globalization is not to conquer the world, but to serve it.

The rapid development of the Internet, the changes of business model, products, and market structures have given rise to new opportunities and transformation to globalization, showing the feature of inclusiveness. Globalization in the future welcomes a new chapter of inclusive sharing.

Why do we define future globalization as one of inclusive sharing? It starts with the characteristics and models of globalization in different stages to compare the differences and variances.

In the past, globalization was the globalization of developed countries and large multinational enterprises. In the future, globalization will get rid of the inequality of participants and become an inclusive globalization in which the disadvantaged groups can directly participate.

Inclusive globalization, which covers a wider range of areas, is a globalization in which all levels of subjects, especially disadvantaged groups, can participate.

In the past, more than 60,000 large-scale multinational enterprises participated in the globalization, while micro, small, and medium sized enterprises were more vulnerable to risks in the international market. It was difficult for them to compete with large enterprises in terms of supplier selection scope, trade channels, and trade negotiations. Often, they were at a disadvantage in the competition.

Cross border e-commerce platform enables SMEs to contact customers at a lower cost, obtain orders, and establish a reputation. Alibaba international station, for example, is dedicated to helping Chinese SMEs to export and global SMEs to expand their overseas markets. Up to now, it has grown into the world's largest international trade platform, with more than 50 million global purchasers registered. On a daily basis, SMEs from more than 200 countries (regions) make procurement and nearly 300,000 inquiries and orders are made there.

The globalization of the past is the one in which low-cost resources and labor forces were plundered and distribution of income was unbalanced; the globalization of the future is the one with mutually beneficial parties and without unequal distribution of interests.

The shared globalization is fairer with wider channels, allowing the disadvantaged groups to obtain better resources and services while achieving win-win results and sharing of interests.

In the past, the vital interests and care for developing countries are often not fully considered in the formulation of international economic and trade rules due to the unequal negotiation abilities between developed countries and developing countries and the unequal weight of voices in the formulation of rules.

With the interconnection of global information and the continuous improvement of network infrastructure, the future globalization not only requires more trade classes and groups to engage in the process of economic globalization, but also strives to create a fairer and more just, more convenient, and more transparent trade process via the Internet, where all participants can benefit from globalization.

The development of Internet and information technology has cast a more profound impact on globalization, and the concept of inclusive sharing is gradually covering all aspects of the global economy. In the future, globalization should be based on equality to ensure that all countries have equal rights, opportunities and rules in international economic cooperation; it should be open-ended without exclusive arrangements to prevent a closed governance mechanism and fragmentation of rules; it should be driven by cooperation, and rules are jointly discussed, mechanisms jointly built, and challenges jointly met; it should be aimed at sharing, and it should be advocated that all participate and all benefit.

In the past, globalization was the trading mode of final products, which differentiated different products by developed and developing countries; in the future, globalization will be a new division of international forces and global value chain model. The division takes place by global producers and consumers as the globalization of global value chain division.

The globalization of global value chain division is to change the trading mode from the final product trade to the value chain trade in increasing relevance and dependence of the industrial structure of all countries. The industrial structure of one country realizes dynamic adjustment and upgrading in the interconnection with other countries' industrial structure, and constantly improves factor allocation efficiency and total factor productivity through resource integration. Therefore, it leads to more efficient production, better service to consumers, and improvement of global development dividend in mutual benefits.

At present, the Internet has opened a new page of globalization with inclusive sharing; in the future, it will bring further development and prosperity of globalization.

\* \* \*

## China plan

At present, globalization is in an unprecedented period of adjustment. New information technology and network facilities promote a new round of the free flow of goods, information, capital, and people. The free flow of these factors has contributed to the new development of globalization and the transformation of traditional industries, bringing historical opportunities for global SMEs. Meanwhile, it has also put forward major challenges and new requirements for the governance of governments and conventional international trade rules.

### *The Belt and Road Initiative*

China enjoys the dividend of globalization development while being constantly committed to promoting the development of inclusive globalization.

China has been actively promoting the Belt and Road Initiative in recent years, which has received a wide response from the international community. In 2017, China's trade volume with countries along the belt road was RMB 7.4 trillion, an increase of 17.8% year-on-year and 3.6% higher than the growth rate of national foreign trade. Among them, the exports amounted to RMB 4.3 trillion, an increase of 12.1%, and the imports RMB, 3.1 trillion an increase of 26.8%; the direct investment of Chinese enterprises to the countries along the belt road was US$14.4 billion, and the newly contracted project amount in the countries along the belt road reached US$144.3 billion, an increase of 14.5% year on year.

The Belt and Road Initiative has become a new engine for China to deepen opening up, expand trade, and drive regional economic development. This is not only a significant practice of building a new pattern of comprehensive opening-up strategy in China, but also an important embodiment of promoting an open, all-encompassing, and inclusive globalization model.

The Belt and Road Initiative is a crucial innovation in China's new global globalization in the background of international economy against globalization. The initiative advocates actively conducting strategic link ups with all countries along the belt road. With trade and investment liberalization and facilitation as a bond, the open mode of infrastructure interconnection, extensive cooperation, and cultural exchanges between different countries is explored. And a new multi-functional and multi-field mutually beneficial cooperation mode including governments, enterprises, social institutions, and civil society is established. The Silk Road Fund, the Asian Investment Bank and the BRICs Development Bank have actively constructed a global free trade area network and contributed China's plan to economic globalization.

The Belt and Road Initiative breaks the bottleneck of the original trade development and provides a new channel for maintaining global efficient and fair trade. Insisting on the principle of co-operation, co-construction, and co-sharing, it has established an integrated and three-dimensional structure in all aspects of investment, financing, production, and network services. It has created a new system platform for communication and integration, allowing more participating countries to create new trade scope through technological exchange and integration, and gradually shift trade facilitation and liberalization from theoretical assumptions into practice.

The Belt and Road Initiative, as China's new window to open up to the outside world, will bring great business opportunities to Chinese enterprises. On the one hand, China has created huge business opportunities for exports; on the other hand, it has played a huge role in promoting the product quality, innovation awareness, and brand awareness of Chinese enterprises.

The Belt and Road Initiative has enabled China's enterprises to go global faster with better quality. Not long ago, the LNG project jointly developed by China, Russia and France was put into operation in the cold Arctic. An enterprise in Qingdao broke through the worldwide problem of insulation of pipelines and equipment in the extremely cold environment of −40°C and sealed a super deal worth RMB 10.1 billion.

With the extension of the Belt and Road Initiative, the E-Road of cross-border e-commerce has also reached more countries and regions, forming the Silk Road online and becoming a new form and important part of international trade. There are more than 200,000 foreign trade enterprises carrying out cross-border e-commerce in China. And the development of cross-border e-commerce has stimulated the strong demand of international railway transportation. Take the China Europe train as an example. In 2017, 3,673 trains were opened, an increase of 116% year on year, exceeding the sum of the past six years. At the same time, since the China Europe train was put under the same brand in 2016, the quality of its operation has been continuously improved, and the value of goods has increased significantly.

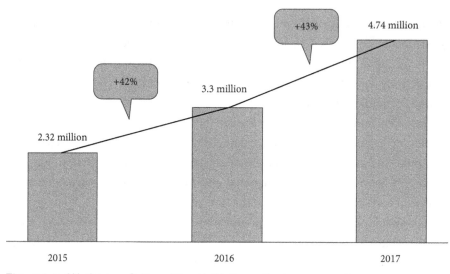

**Figure 1.4** Alibaba.com Belt and Road Initiative active buyers growth

Cross-border e-commerce platform, as one of the infrastructures of digital silk road, shoulders the major responsibility of convenience for trade. The platform data also reflects the trade activeness of the countries along the belt. It is shown that the number of active buyers in the belt countries was 43% higher in 2017 than the previous year and 11% higher than the number of active buyers in the whole website (excluding China), according to the data on Alibaba international station.

The Belt and Road Initiative countries' cross-border e-commerce connectivity index[1]

Alibaba prepared the E-commerce Connectivity Index (ECI) for the Belt and Road Initiative countries according to the big data of cross-border e-commerce (including cross-border e-commerce retail exports and imports). The ECI index is designed to reflect the degree of connectivity between China and the belt and road countries in cross-border e-commerce trade.

The higher the export index, the more "made in China" goods the country purchases; the higher the import index, the more goods from the country Chinese consumers purchase.

1. Source: *The One-year Report of the Belt and Road Initiative Cross Border Business Opportunities* of the Ali Research Institute in 2017.

According to the ECI of belt road countries, which is prepared according to Alibaba's cross border e-commerce big data:

- Eastern Europe, Western Asia and ASEAN countries are most closely connected with China's cross-border e-commerce.
- Top 10 countries with the highest ECI with China are: Russia, Israel, Thailand, Ukraine, Poland, Czech Republic, Moldova, Turkey, Belarus, and Singapore.
- Regarding exports, global AliExpress covers all the Belt and Road Initiative countries, and 45% of the buyers are from those countries, of which Russia, Ukraine, Israel, Belarus and Poland are with the top five countries of purchasing power.

### Government assistance

The Chinese government attaches great importance to the development of cross-border e-commerce as a new engine of China's economic development, a new format of industrial transformation and a new window of opening up in the new era.

From 2012 to 2017, China successively issued more than 20 policies and documents. Among them, there are nine policy documents issued by the State Council and the general office of the State Council (3 directly by the State Council and 6 directly by the General Office of the State Council), which provide strong support for the development of "E-road" cross-border e-commerce from the national strategy and policy level.

In March 2015, the State Council approved the establishment of China (Hangzhou) cross-border e-commerce comprehensive pilot area. In 2016, to deepen reform and opening up and explore the benefit of that, the State Council supported the pilot cross-border e-commerce comprehensive pilot areas in 12 cities, including Tianjin, Shanghai, Chongqing, Zhengzhou, etc. And they helped solve the problems that occur in the process of cross-border e-commerce development through a series of policies and systems. As a result, replicable and generalizable experience to promote cross-border e-commerce across the country can be provided as well as new support for the development of foreign trade with new models. In May 2016, the State Council issued several opinions on promoting the stability and improvement of foreign trade and put forward 14 policies and measures to promote the development of cross-border e-commerce from five aspects.[1]

Guided by the state's major policies, provincial and municipal governments are also actively seeking institutional innovation and cooperation between government and enterprises to achieve the transformation of new and old driving forces with the help of cross-border e-commerce.

Cross border e-commerce has the features of fragmentation, small amounts, and high-frequency. What if the original supervision does not adapt to the changes of trade pattern?

The Hangzhou municipal government is the first to promote institutional innovation in China. How to identify the regulatory subject? Hangzhou took the lead in trying to create the B2B recognition standard in China and formed various supervision modes such as customs B2C import, B2C export, bonded export, etc. based on different recognition. How to solve the disputes faced by cross-border e-commerce? In accordance with the arbitration management of international commercial disputes, the city has set up an Internet court and an Internet arbitration alliance to promote Internet arbitration in the Asia Pacific region. How to guarantee the quality of cross-border e-commerce? It has founded the first cross-border retail commodity quality monitoring center in the country. At present, it mainly monitors the cross-border retail import with the Alibaba platform, and will be promoted to export products in the future.

On November 27, 2017, 14 departments, including the Ministry of Commerce, issued a letter on the mature experience and practices formed in the exploration of the cross-border e-commerce comprehensive pilot area. It requires local governments to copy and promote the experience and practices of six systems, including information sharing, financial services, intelligent logistics, e-commerce credit, statistical monitoring, and risk prevention and control, as well as those of online single window and offline comprehensive parks. The core structure and

---

1. The first is to encourage financial institutions to loan to enterprises engaged in foreign trade with orders and benefits; the second is to improve processing trade policies, comprehensively apply treasury, land, and financial policies, and support the transfer of processing trade to the central and western regions; the third is to underpin enterprises to establish an international marketing network system, and encourage them to set up an overseas service guarantee system; the fourth is to develop and expand cross-border e-commerce and market procurement trade pilot projects; the fifth is to reduce the average export inspection rate and strengthen classified guidance.

experience of "six systems and two platforms" in Hangzhou comprehensive pilot area have been greatly accepted.

In addition, with the help of government resources, traditional manufacturing enterprises and the majority of SMEs cooperate with the platform to jointly launch a series of project cooperation, which has become a new mode of regional transformation and development.

Taking Shandong as an example, on December 26, 2017, the Shandong provincial government and Alibaba Group signed a comprehensive strategic cooperation agreement in Jinan to promote the transformation of new and old driving forces. The two parties will first take the Alibaba international station as the base and jointly carry out new foreign trade cooperation through the implementation of "excellent business and excellent product selection project." Consequently, this shall promote the transformation and development of foreign trade in Shandong Province and the transformation of new and old driving forces of economy.

Relying on the cooperation between government and enterprises, Shandong's SMEs have welcomed a new opportunity for commodities to go beyond the seas. How should the SMEs without foreign trade experience operate? Alibaba international station launched special activities, offline training, and online platform support to help Shandong foreign trade enterprises grow rapidly. What about the lack of resources for brand operation? The Alibaba international station spares no effort to promote specific projects such as cross-border e-commerce B2B Shandong brand going abroad, rapid cross-border sales of Shandong goods, etc., provide website resources for key industries and enterprises, and stimulates high-quality growth of import and export business of SMEs.

With the support of the policy, China's manufacturing enterprises and brands have become faster, more efficient, and lower cost to carry out foreign trade business. This not only helps the development of SMEs, increases local employment opportunities, but also realizes transformation and upgrading through e-commerce, expands the global market, and builds China's global brand.

> **CASE STUDIES**   The Linyi mode of government assistance in foreign trade
> transformation

How can the government contribute to the development of new foreign trade? Linyi City Government in Shandong Province has presented an effective Linyi mode.

On the basis of Alibaba's data application + localization service, the government has established a multi-party linkage among the government, foreign trade platform enterprises, ecological third parties, and Linyi foreign trade enterprises. It aimed to push the "physical link" of the new foreign trade to undergo "chemical changes," to help Linyi's micro, small, and medium sized enterprises to more easily realize their dream of globalization, and to accelerate the layout of the significant keystones of eWTP.

Linyi city is a famous logistics capital in China, whose logistics network covers 1,800 outlets at or above the county level and radiates more than 30 countries and regions around the world. However, the foreign trade business of Linyi, despite the advantages of logistics in trade, is not as thriving as domestic trade. Under the new circumstances of transformation of new and old driving forces of the country and further opening up, Linyi Municipal government took the lead in testing the transformation of foreign trade and became the one of the first cities in China to enter a strategic cooperation framework agreement with Alibaba in 2017.

Relying on Alibaba's resources and technical strength, Linyi's new foreign trade journey has thus begun.

The transformation of foreign trade is primarily the transformation of the minds of traders, so that potential trade participants can better understand, adapt to, and accept the mode of "Internet plus foreign trade." For this reason, Linyi Municipal Government jointly held the framework agreement press conference with Alibaba to introduce and promote new foreign trade concepts and models as warming up. The first step of the transformation of foreign trade was thus taken.

The new media, with a greater impact on the public's cognition, is more likely to cause social repercussions. With the support of the Linyi Municipal Bureau of Commerce, Linyi TV station, and Alibaba SME international trade business department were the first in China to record a foreign trade reality show. The first season of the program consists of four episodes. Six unique representatives of new foreign businessmen narrated their successful mode of going global and the compelling stories of foreign trade development. To the country, the dream of medium-sized enterprises going global was encouraged. More than 600 on-the-spot recording tickets were sold out in three days, and over 700 foreign trade enterprises showed up. Through multiple rounds of prime time broadcasting on TV, the social effect was greater, allowing these excellent models to evolve from mere words to vivid stories, thus reaching the hearts of audiences all over the

**Program value**

- Six short documentaries of foreign traders (produced by the TV station for free)
- Output of six new export modes
- Release of four dimensions of new foreign trade (e-commerce dimension, data dimension, operation dimension and development dimension)
- [new foreign trade service day] launch of regional diagnostic activities

**Figure 1.5** Linyi foreign trade reality show

country. They truly felt the changes of Linyi's foreign trade transformation and discovery of new opportunities and approaches for foreign trade. It has contributed greatly to the upgrading of the mental transformation mode of traders.

After the change of understanding of a new direction, how to do it next has become a common concern. The offline diagnostic salon of Linyi new foreign trade service day has solved the problem of how. Potential foreign traders can participate in offline experience sharing and expert lecturing activities organized by Alibaba in the form of TV and WeChat QR code. The session contains a small group of 40 to 50 learners so as to effectively realize the training and transformation from potential foreign traders to qualified foreign traders. Through learning, they gradually realized that foreign trade is not as difficult as they expected before. As long as there is a certain trade experience, one can solve many problems in the trade chain through Alibaba's one-stop service. Therefore, the confidence and determination to explore and try new foreign trade are built.

In addition to basic cultivation, there is also support for the excellent. With the endorsement and promotion of the Linyi Municipal government, the "promotion conference of excellent commercial products" in nine counties, three districts of Linyi City have also received strong support from all walks of life. With the help of the transformation of new and old driving forces in Shandong Province, the project of making excellent commercial products has taken place in Linyi. More than 3,000 people participated in more than a dozen events. The new foreign trade concept was deeply popular through this sinking-style promotion, and the concept of high-quality development has been more precisely popularized.

In the process, what if there are some perplexing questions? Enterprises can access to online Q&A at any time through Alibaba customer service center, turn to the Language Lecturer Group for help on Linyi opening day, and receive offline training at fixed points on a regular basis; what if there is a lack of talents during the development of foreign trade? More than ten mutual selections for enterprises and VIPs have been held to export foreign trade talents to Linyi foreign trade enterprises. These online and offline activities jointly played the symphony of Linyi's new foreign trade transformation.

Since the signing of the strategic framework agreement over a year ago, the Linyi Municipal government has been turning every promise on paper into a real activity, summit, and salon, and has built a model room for foreign trade in Linyi. In the future, the city will take the industry as a point to break through the advantageous industries such as construction machinery, willow crafts, and construction plates. The goal is to open the supply chain through data precipitation service + local supporting services and accelerate its integration into the eWTP and the global trading system. At the same time, the local government will accelerate the layout in such areas as preferential policies for excellent products, optimization of online trade processes, etc., so as to help local enterprises more efficiently realize the new foreign trade transformation and promote the higher quality development of Linyi economy.

### Trade rules in the new era: eWTP

Cross border e-commerce is becoming an essential form of international trade, and SMEs are gradually becoming the main body of it. However, there are no real international rules for them. With the coming of the era of fragmentation, individuation, customization, and the short and small simplification of international trade, they urgently ask for a free, fair, and open trade platform that belongs to them. Therefore, eWTP came into being.

The concept of eWTP (electronic world trade platform) was proposed by Jack Ma, chairman of Alibaba Group's board of directors in 2016. Simply put, it is to create opportunities for young people and SMEs to participate in global free trade by establishing a platform. It calls for following the current trend of the rapid development of the digital economy, promoting the global inclusive trade and the growth of the digital economy, and incubating the new rules of global trade in the Internet era.

eWTP is a private sector led, market driven, open, and transparent public-private partnership platform with multi stakeholder involved. It is the basis for SMEs to re-establish trade rules in the global scope. It can simplify the channels to consumers and greatly reduce the trade costs of SMEs. The threshold for SMEs to participate in the global value chain will correspondingly be reduced. In addition, through the application of online payment tools, it can also help SMEs' cash flow and working capital.

The eWTP ecosystem consists of three layers: the rule layer, the business layer and the technology layer.

The first is the rule layer. All stakeholders jointly explore and incubate new rules and standards in the digital era, such as digital customs border, tax policy, data flow, credit system, consumer protection, etc., which are directly pertinent to e-commerce.

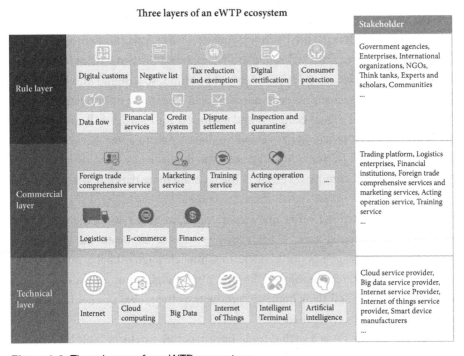

**Figure 1.6** Three layers of an eWTP ecosystem

The second is the business layer. All relevant parties carry out business exchanges and cooperation related to digital economy and e-commerce, and establish a new infrastructure in the Internet era, such as an e-commerce platform, financial payments, logistics and warehousing, comprehensive foreign trade services, marketing, education, and training, etc.

The third is the technology layer. The technical architecture of eWTP based on the Internet, big data and cloud computing, the Internet of things, artificial intelligence, etc. is jointly established.

These three layers are closely related and dependent on each other. The discussion of the rule layer mainly comes from the practice of the business layer and the technology layer, and its results and consensus will promote the business cooperation of the digital economy and the innovation and development of new technologies.

Since the proposal of eWTP, it has been positively responded to and highly recognized by international organizations, government agencies, business circles, and think tank scholars, including UN agencies. In September 2016, as a core policy proposal of G20 business activities (B20), the eWTP initiative was written into the communiqué of G20 leaders' Hangzhou summit.

On March 22, 2017, Jack Ma, chairman of the board of directors of Alibaba group, and Najib Razak, then-Prime Minister of Malaysia, announced that the first eWTP pilot area was established in Malaysia, and the two parties jointly built the digital free trade area (eHub). eHub will be built into a digital hub integrating logistics, payments, customs clearance, and data, becoming an infrastructure for the development of digital economy and a window for micro, small, and medium sized micro enterprises in Malaysia and Southeast Asia to enter the world. At the same time, the real transaction and credit data deposited by these overseas small and medium-sized enterprises can help them obtain more data empowerment and funding.

On October 30, 2017, the first export order of SMEs was received in the Malaysia experimental area; a Malaysian enterprise exported the first semi-finished pacifiers worth about US$900 to China through Alibaba international station and OneTouch, becoming the first eWTP digital hub outside China. It helped local SMEs sell their domestic products to the global market for the first time through the Internet channel.

Behind the eWTP is a digital trade infrastructure platform built by Alibaba, mainly supported by businesses of Alibaba B2B business groups such as

**Figure 1.7** Establishment of the Malaysia eHub

international station and OneTouch. The increasing enhancement of the platform has played a role of reassurance for WTO to embrace e-commerce and SMEs. In the past, multinational companies mainly relied on sales representatives to expand their sales networks around the world, but now through cross-border B2B e-commerce platforms such as the Alibaba international station, they can extend their sales and service radius to the global market efficiently and cheaply. At the same time, it can also absorb excellent SMEs into its global supply chain system through the Internet.

As Xi Jinping, President of the PRC, put it at the Davos forum in the 2017, "The world economy is no longer a one-man show. We exist with and within each other. Only joining the wave of global economy can a country step out of economic distress and achieve economic sustainable development. The sea holds water from all rivers. Inclusive economy has become the direction of the world economy development."

SMEs account for 90% of the total global business and more than 50% of the employment.[1] They play an important role in promoting global employment, job creation, investment, innovation and economic growth. The first mover advantage

1. Source: The implementation framework of G20 small and medium-sized enterprises financing action plan released at the G20 summit in 2016.

of Chinese enterprises in B2B cross-border E-commerce makes SMEs, which were not heeded by the international community, become the makers of international e-commerce standards and rules.

"In the next 30 years, I bet that there will be six million or 60 million companies participating in the globalization, and I'm sure that we will make it happen," Jack Ma predicted at the 2018 Davos forum, and the global buying and selling of small and medium-sized enterprises is coming true step by step.

**CASE STUDIES**  Malaysia digital free trade area (eHub)

In the Malaysia pilot area, Alibaba B2B business group mainly provides three levels of services.

First, OneTouch and Cainiao Network provide services in foreign trade such as logistics, customs declarations, foreign exchange collections, foreign exchange settlements, and settlement to Malaysian SMEs with export needs.

Second, the international station provides Malaysian enterprises with information display, transactions, credit guarantees, and supply chain financial services, so that they can improve efficiency, reduce costs, and realize online transaction.

Third, credit assurance service is made available. Next, credit assurance products will be launched in Malaysia.

Alibaba B2B platform can not only provide SMEs with customs clearance, logistics, foreign exchange, tax refunds, finance and other import and export services, but also help local small- and medium-sized sellers to consolidate bulk orders, so that their goods can also be packed on ships and airplanes through the combination of orders.

Originally, they were looking for one-to-one single point basic service providers. With the "single window" mode provided by Alibaba B2B, they could gather a large number of export orders and form an intensive service advantage.

These efforts have greatly increased the efficiency of Malaysia's SMEs to carry out global trade, and they can enjoy technological and intensive dividends in cross-border, customs clearance, and exchange settlements, as well as guaranteed international trade services.

# CHAPTER II

# The Evolution of Foreign Trade in the DT Era

A S A NEW PRODUCTIVITY, technological transformation is imperceptibly catalyzing the change of lifestyle and production mode, which gives rise to the change of business form and organization structure, which further formulates new requirements for enterprise transformation and human capability.

The Internet, the mobile Internet, big data, and other technological revolutions have driven social changes in all respects. However, unbalanced and inadequate development is widespread in the new round of productivity versus production relations contest in foreign trade.

\* \* \*

## Data Technology (DT), the Fourth Technological Revolution

The global economy continues growing, but the leading giants are changing. Let's take a look at the top 10 companies on the global market capitalization list in 2017.[1]

---

1. Source: Quoted from the top 100 global enterprise market value published by Lishi Business Review on January 28, 2018.

1.  Apple, with a market value of US$885.88 billion, of the consumer electronics industry;
2.  Alphabet, the parent company of Google, with a market value of US$825.105 billion, of the Internet industry;
3.  Microsoft, with a market value of US$725.714 billion, of the Internet industry;
4.  Amazon, with a market value of US $675.609 billion, of the Internet industry;
5.  Tencent Holdings, with a market value of US$572.475 billion, of the Internet industry;
6.  Facebook, with a market value of US$551.797 billion, of the Internet industry;
7.  Berkshire Hathaway, with a market value of US$536.3 billion, of the insurance industry;
8.  Alibaba, with a market value of US$525.6 billion, of the Internet industry;
9.  JPMorgan Chase, with a market value of US$403,596 billion, of the banking industry;
10. Industrial and Commercial Bank of China, with a market value of US$390,066 billion, of the banking industry.

It can be noticed that JPMorgan Chase, a financial giant that has dominated the United States for a century, Berkshire Hathaway, the evergreen financial investment company founded by Warren Buffett, the master of investment, and the Industrial and Commercial Bank of China, which is nicknamed "the largest bank in the universe" by Chinese netizens, made the cut on the list. What also deserves to be noticed is that, in addition to these three financial enterprises, the other seven are technology giants, five of which occupy the Top five seats. Google, Amazon, Facebook, Tencent, and Alibaba, typical Internet companies that could not be more familiar, cover half of the list.

Let's time travel to a decade ago. In 2007, the world's most valuable companies were ExxonMobil, General Electric, Microsoft, Industrial and Commercial Bank of China, Citigroup, AT&T, Royal Dutch Shell, Bank of America, PetroChina, and China Mobile. Nowadays, these industrial giants have been surpassed by Internet companies one after another. These great changes fully illustrate the great power brought by the Internet, in whose era, market value has replaced income and profit to become the best measurement of enterprise value and future growth potential.

Human beings have stepped into the era of the digital economy. The advancement of technology is more than a single point of application, but the change of infrastructure penetrating all aspects of life from the industrial age to the information age, from the IT age to the DT era. It goes beyond the changes in lifestyle and the production factor. Gradually, "PC +" has developed to "Internet +", and "cable +" to "wireless +." The digital economy is spread all over production, work, and life. Data shows what news to read, what products to buy, what markets to open up, and how to develop business. The new trade mode and business form has become the social landscape of DT era.

### Technology upgrading: IT to DT resources

A look back on the history of scientific and technological progress and modern human history illuminates that technology is the driving force to promote social progress and constantly reshape business forms.

The first scientific and technological revolution, as the release of physical strength, enabled human strength to be stronger. The steam engine was invented. And the large-scale mechanized production factory replaced the original self-sufficient family workshop, freeing human physical strength. This marked the transition from agricultural civilization to industrial civilization.

The second, as a harness of energy, enabled human beings to go further. In this stage, the generator gradually replaced the steam engine as a new power source, making full use of power technology. This promoted the concentration of production and capital, and the development of modern enterprises.

The third is a revolution of information control technology. The rapid development of microcomputers contributed greatly to the wide use of electronics. The past revolutions in science and technology have pushed forward the continuous development of production technology, but this one has also borne fruit in the continuous improvement of the quality and skills of workers and a more efficient global exchange of information and resources.

This time, we will move from the IT age to the DT (data technology) era. The application of big data, cloud computing, the Internet, and intelligent terminals have made data individuals' essentials, enterprises' production means, and future economic society's new infrastructure like water, electricity, and oil.

As an important milestone of human progress, every technological revolution certainly generates a certain impact on the traditional production relations. The harness of data has not only greatly promoted the transformation of human social economy, politics, and culture, but also influenced and changed the way of life and thinking of human beings. Significant changes have also taken place in all aspects of human daily life, such as clothing, food, housing, transportation, and daily usage. The future productivity is the ability of calculation and innovation based on data.

### Role Transformation: from production domination to demand-driven

The development of productive forces involves the adaptation of production relations. In the DT era, the first is the transformation of human thinking patterns. To understand this change, it must start with the difference between IT and DT.

The first difference is that they play different roles.

In the IT era, the problem of information asymmetry is solved with information nodes as the center. Tools enable people to access to rich information as they lowered bar of the access and consequently eliminate the information gap, thus eliminating the problems due to information asymmetry.

Take business as an example. What the Alibaba international station completed was to turn the offline business online, thus eliminating the information gap between sellers and buyers. Pictures and product information are made available, and one click of search can easily compare the prices of similar products, therefore a smaller chance of being deceived. And rare products such as left-handed tools and large size clothes can be quickly found. Based on information technology, we have conveniently established a bridge to enhance understanding and expanded the information set of judgments and decisions.

But this is a centralized information model that eliminates information asymmetry without breaking the imbalance between supply and demand. A supplier is found, but can it supply personalized components? A client is found on the other side of the earth, but is the waterproof wig really suitable for those who fancy swimming and surfing all day long? In the end, the products fail to meet the personalized needs of a customer, and the application of IT cannot change the imbalance between supply and demand. By means of information matching, the contradiction between supply and demand of products and services cannot be fundamentally eradicated.

In the DT era, as the Alibaba international station began to change from an information platform to a trading platform, data provides means for supply-side reform. Light is thrown upon the solution of the problem as there is the gradual change from production domination to demand driven.

Compared with the one common requirement from thousands of customers in the information age, it is the thousands of requirements from them. Personalized demand brings great challenges to product supply, but information technology cannot fundamentally solve the imbalance between them. Personalized demand is colossal with plenty of forms, but supply is determined by production. Information media and platforms can reduce supply and demand friction, but they can never completely match them. For example, have a product online allows more to know that there is such a product, but it doesn't mean that it is going to be needed. Therefore, it is necessary to have DT thinking to fundamentally change the demand-supply pattern.

The solution is to dynamically present the whole demand information. In 2017, the popular color was purple. Everyone was crazy about the video game *Arena of Valor*. President trump twitted the word "covfefe". So twitter immediately launched a word guessing event, and big data showed that covfefe was trending on

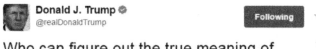

**Figure 2.1** Trump invented the word "covfefe" on twitter

**Figure 2.2** "Covfefe" hot products

top. Life is like a series of trump tweets. "You never know what is the next one you are going to get" went viral at the time. The Internet traffic Trump, as President of America has triggered, together with the unlimited imagination and entertaining effect, has inspired designers. And voila, a business opportunity was seized.

Through intelligent data analysis, suppliers can quickly respond to current hot spots and demands. Based on big data technology analysis and market forecast, they further adjust and change product design and supply, and achieve the overall supply-demand matching through "intelligent manufacturing." In addition, in-depth data support makes it possible to customize in accordance with thousands of requirements. Retailors can recommend products according to the buyer's age, region, focus area, discount preference, and other labels, which greatly improved the transaction success rate.

Obviously, the change of product supply meets the personalized demand of the buyer, creates the demand of the buyer while realizing the transformation from production domination to demand driven, and from manufacturing to intelligent manufacturing.

### Thinking Transformation: From Self-centered to Mutual Benefit and Equality

*The second difference between IT and DT is the thinking pattern.*

In the IT era, information is self-centered, and information releaser and information user are two completely different roles. For example, when a merchant releases a product, he/she is the releaser of the information, which is accepted and used by online buyers. If he/she wants to change the acceptance and competitiveness of the merchandise, only the product line and product style can be changed by the merchants themselves, or the types and channels of product release be increased. This approach is a lonely fight, and each step of progress needs to be driven by his/her own strength.

In the era, buyers/commodity data users have become producers and contributors of transaction and commodity big data. Static information supply has become dynamic information interaction. For example, in addition to investing in a large number of intelligent bicycles, Mobi Bike, a bike-sharing enterprise also records the riding routes of every consumer who uses its bicycles through the navigation and positioning device installed on the bike. It makes social forces become real-time and dynamic commuting information, consumption information, and traffic information providers. The traffic information of bicycle sharing comes from the spontaneous supply of the public, which greatly improves the cost and efficiency. Through the dynamic processing and application of the big data of shared bicycle, it provides a basis for bicycle launches and public transport equipment supply in turn. This both solves the public "last kilometer" commuting problem, and forms intelligent traffic planning, which truly realizes "one for all and all for one."

The information supply in the IT era is internalized and closed. As a centralized information service, it enables the government and large enterprises to play a leading role in the economic and social development. In the DT era, information supply is more altruistic, sharing and decentralized, and more open and transparent. The powerful computing power in the DT era will stimulate the creativity of both large and small enterprises while constantly exploiting the social value of information.

*　*　*

## Three New Trends of Foreign Trade Development

The mode of foreign trade driven by Internet is constantly changing. At present, cross-border trade shows three trends: multinational, wireless, and online.

### *Multinational*

The Internet propels the development of inclusive trade, which is fully reflected in the subject of trade. In the past, western countries were traditional trading powers, accounting for over half of the world's trade. At present, small countries have witnessed a boost in the order volume with the help of Internet. The global trade has become multinational.

Take the Alibaba international station as an example. In 2017, the international station's daily traffic of tens of millions of buyers came from over 200 countries, and the number of global buyers increased by 28% year on year. Among them, the United States ranked first, accounting for 19%; India second, accounting for 7%; the third and fourth places were taken by the UK and Canada, accounting for around 4%; Russia, Australia, and Brazil came next, accounting for around 3%; the proportion gap between these top countries was shrinking.

In terms of growth rate, the countries with the fastest growth rate of active buyers are India, Vietnam, and Nepal, with growth rates of 87%, 75%, and 74%. Multi-nationalization also makes different requirements for goods and services: suppliers in small- and medium-sized countries should gradually break the pattern

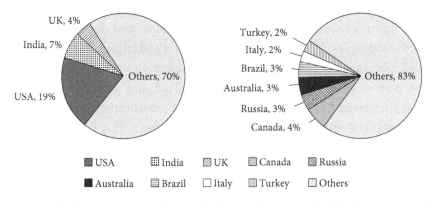

**Figure 2.3** Traffic distribution of tens of millions of buyers in the Alibaba international station

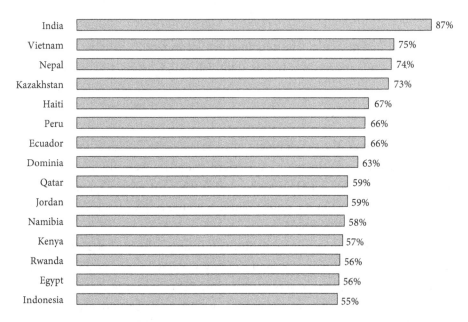

**Figure 2.4** Top 15 countries with the biggest year-on-year increase in the number of active buyers on Alibaba international station and their growth rate

of sole focus on English websites and pay more attention to the layout of various local languages in terms of language talent cultivation and resource allocation. The business opportunity was presented thank to the cultivation and upgrading of the port mode used by countries that speak less commonly used languages. Time consuming as it is, it is going to be worth the efforts.

### Wireless

In 2017, the transaction volume of Tmall's "double 11" reached RMB 168.2 billion, an increase of 39.4% year-on-year, of which the wireless terminal accounted for 90%, while that in 2016 and 2015 accounted for 82% and 68% respectively. When the traditional consumption has changed to be completed on wireless terminals, this trend will inevitably happen to the foreign trade.

With the development of the Internet, there are many traffic entrances, and wireless is an important trend.

The number of wireless users is growing at an alarming rate. By comparing the growth rate of wireless end users and PC end users of the Alibaba international station in 2015 and 2016, we have noticed that the growth rate of wireless end users is much higher than that of PC end users. In 2016, the growth rate reached 90%, proving the gradually mobile trade mode. Compared with the end of 2017 and 2016, the number of users visiting Alibaba international station on the PC end

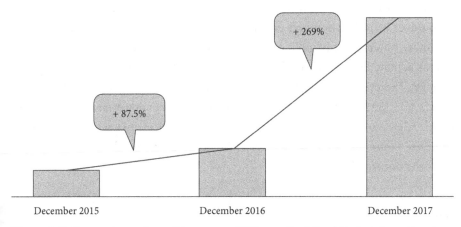

**Figure 2.5** Comparison of monthly average DAU growth of the Alibaba international station wireless terminal (APP) on a year-on-year basis

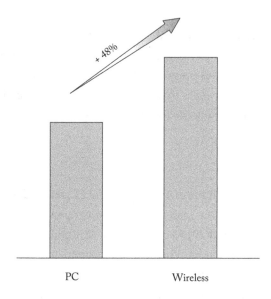

**Figure 2.6** Comparison of activeness between wireless end buyers and PC end buyers of Alibaba international station

decreased by 29% while that of active buyers on the App end increased by 52% year on year, and that of daily active users (DAU) increased by 269% year-on-year. Many buyers will visit alibaba.com from both PC and wireless terminals, of whom more only adopt wireless terminals. The large growth of wireless users reflects the characteristics of younger trading groups and fragmented trading time.

Wireless users are more active. App end being more concise and clearer encourages buyer's action and enhances the wireless ordering experience. More and more buyers use the mobile phone as the foreign trade purchasing port. The buyer's activity level using wireless devices is 48% higher than that of PC end on average. The purchase behavior of wireless buyers is different from that of PC buyers. For the seller, it will be the key point for the future enterprise to pay attention to the release of wireless products and product services, use wireless scenes to complete communication with wireless buyer, and explore their characteristics and behavior trends.

### Online

Traditional trade links, unnecessarily long, include suppliers, exporters, importers, distributors at all levels, super retailers, and overseas buyers. The Internet makes it

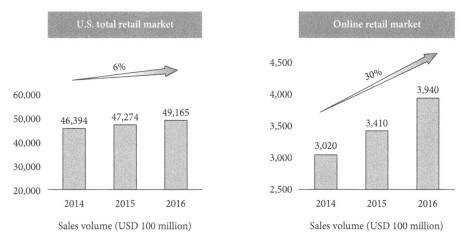

**Figure 2.7** Data changes in the U.S. total retail market and online retail market

easier for more buyers from all over the world to contact Chinese manufacturers, thus driving the "de-intermediation" of the entire trade link.

Take the United States as an example. The total volume of the retail market in the United States is colossal with annual sales of nearly $5 trillion and an annual growth rate of 6% for the overall retail market. Correspondingly, the online retail market in the United States is growing rapidly with an annual growth rate of about 15%, far higher than that of the retail market. In addition, the total number of online sellers in the United States is about 10 million and the target group of retailers with cross-border purchase demand is more than one million. The cross-border purchase volume surpasses US$30 billion. The online power is taking center stage.

In the online mode, retailers who used to purchase goods from wholesalers now search for goods directly via the Internet and purchase them directly from Chinese suppliers, skipping the originally lengthy traditional link. This kind of online process also brings a greater variety of products for retailers: direct access to more abundant products from source countries and even the possibility to order personalized products.

In the future, de-intermediation will flatten the sales channels. Buyers from Chinese suppliers will change from importers, wholesalers, and distributors to terminal retailers. This will alter the characteristics of commodities into small and single with high frequency and larger volume. The retail market will dominate the global consumer market.

How to increase the order quantity? The key is found in receipts and returns. The corporate brand and reputation will become the passport of future business. Suppliers need to make corresponding adjustments in goods, service capacity, and production capacity.

*   *   *

## New technology reconstructs the form of foreign trade

The mode and concept of the DT era is gradually pushing the change of international trade forms. The cutting-edge technologies such as artificial intelligence, the Internet of things, VR (virtual reality) / AR (augmented reality) have come to the majority of consumers. They have brought great changes to people's lifestyle while impacting work style and efficiency.

With the explosive development of global e-commerce, major changes have taken place in the main body and form of international trade, business models, and organization mode, and gradually subvert traditional trade.

Regarding traditional foreign trade, the form can be summarized as "container, "chain" and "human relationships."

(1) In the form of "container" foreign trade, multinational companies are the main participants. In the traditional way of foreign trade, they play an important role with their resource advantages. With their absolute say in foreign trade, it tends to be large-scale and homogeneous. At the same time, it is done at large trade amount and low frequency. Large containers are the main carrier of goods trade.

(2) The "chain" foreign trade pattern has many trade processes and long links. The entire process of traditional foreign trade is completed offline from order placement, delivery, customs declaration to settlement of foreign exchange. Only after the distribution of domestic and foreign trade companies and dealers can the goods reach the buyer from the manufacturer. The chain link is long and slow and international trade is a long straight-line chain.

(3) "Human relationships" form of foreign trade is a mutually competitive foreign trade. In traditional foreign trade, an intermediate trader can only serve a

few manufacturers and sell products to a wholesaler. Human relationships are the main way to keep customers. At the same time, different foreign trade companies compete with each other and low price is the main competitive advantage.

Under the transformation of new technology, the traditional mode of foreign trade is gradually being reconstructed.

### *The Morphological Characteristics of Small Yet Beautiful*

In the DT era, the small yet beautiful foreign trade pattern is gradually changing the original container typed foreign trade pattern as an injection of new vitality into foreign trade. This small yet beautiful includes the following aspects:

The subject of purchase and sale is small yet beautiful. A large number of SMEs, even individual businesses sell products to all over the world on the Internet platform, which is in sharp contrast to the traditional global trade dominated by large enterprises and trading companies. These small yet beautiful enterprises put an end to the monopoly of transnational enterprises in the global supply chain and participate in global business activities directly and equally. An increasing number of young people and small enterprises with pioneering spirit will play an important role in global economic trade and employment innovation. On the other hand, global buyers also exhibit the trend of "small yet beautiful." According to the sampling survey data of Alibaba international station, small buyers account for 85% of total buyers, of which micro buyers account for 74%.

---

**CASE STUDIES**  Cross-border trade market trends – taking Alibaba international station as an example

---

According to the user data of the Alibaba international station and relevant sampling survey, the overall cross-border trade market exhibits three market trends:

- The proportion of retailers and wholesalers increased. Retailers and wholesalers account for 46%, factories for 21% and trading companies for 20%.

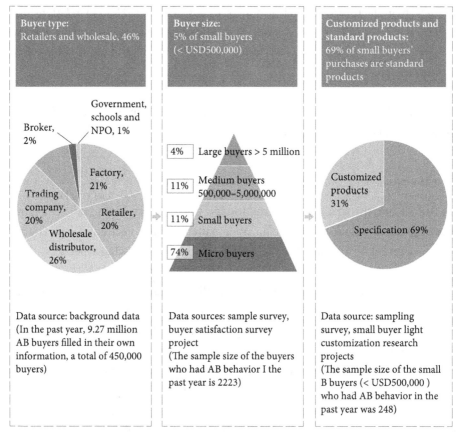

**Figure 2.8** Overall cross-border trade market trend of Alibaba international station

*Source: Alibaba international station user data and relevant sampling survey*

- Miniaturization of buyers. The proportion of small buyers with a transaction volume smaller than US$500,000 is 85%. The proportion of medium-sized buyers is 11% while the that of large buyers whose transaction volume surpasses US$5 million is only 4%. The miniaturization of buyer scale leads to the change of buyer sourcing habits.
- Specifications account for a high proportion of product requirement. 69% of small buyers(small B) purchases are standard products, and 31% of them are customized products.

The trade content is "small yet beautiful." With the rise of the Internet and mobile Internet, enterprises have gradually engaged in online trade from offline trade. The proportion of cross-border e-commerce in international trade has surged. Younger buyers and more wireless transactions at fragmented time have characterized international trade as small and single with a high frequency and personalized customization. In the era of miniaturization and fragmentation, the total amount of orders will not decrease. It is that following the change of trade and trade patterns, the orders will be split. Similarly, if there are dozens or even hundreds of orders, a supplier can still have the say of the channel.

**CASE STUDIES**   New image of overseas buyers

According to the questionnaire survey of the Alibaba international station users, overseas furniture shopping is characterized as:

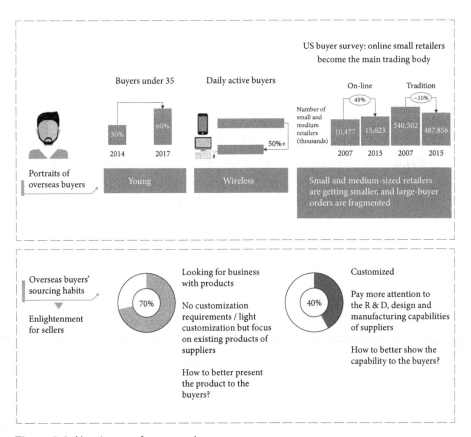

**Figure 2.9** New image of overseas buyers

*Source: Alibaba international station user survey*

- Young. In 2014, buyers under the age of 35 accounted for 30%, while in 2017, the proportion rose to 60%, doubling in three years.
- Wireless. Among the daily active buyers, the number of users using mobile Internet is 50% higher than that using PC.
- Miniaturized. In the survey of American buyers, online small retailers have become the main body of trade. Among the investigated buyers, the number of online small- and medium-sized retailers in 2015 was 15.623 million, about 49% higher than 10.477 million in 2007; while the number of traditional small- and medium-sized retailers continued to decrease, about 488 million in 2015, 10% lower than 541 million in 2007. The characteristics of fragmentation of large orders and gradual miniaturization of orders began to exhibit.

The organizational structure is "small yet beautiful." In terms of organizational structure and operation mode, enterprises can flexibly set up digital departments according to their own business situation and the degree of digital transformation and solve the coordination problem of functional departments through organizational structure optimization. In terms of operation mode, data is relied upon to explore new product demand trends and technology trends while paying more attention to the platform and small team's quick response to market changes; with the vertical analysis of the Internet, the use of big data, and the sensitivity of small teams, every enterprise has the chance to become number one in the world and achieve global fame, which was unimaginable in the past.

Iterative innovation is small yet beautiful. Artificial intelligence, big data, cloud computing, and other technologies enable enterprises to start with "small data" to continuously improve the application ability of data in business operations. Taking artificial intelligence as an example, the National Federation of Independent Business (NFIB) disclosed that SMEs have begun to pay attention to this trend, and 59% of them are actively understanding and responding to the changes that artificial intelligence may bring to enterprise management. Through the continuous iteration of "small innovation" in brand exploitation, efficiency improvement, and consumption experience, the enterprise gradually forms its own individual competitiveness. In the era of miniaturization, with the help of big data, the products delivered by sellers will be more varied. On the one hand, they can determine the style according to customer requirements and carry out micro customizations; on the other hand, they can also innovate products to better meet customer needs.

**CASE STUDIES**  Alibaba's technical empowerment

- *Communication without borders*

At the CES (International Consumer Electronics Show) in January 2018, the Alibaba international station made a live display of an AI real-time interpretation tool, attracting the attention of thousands of participants. At present, Alibaba Group's machine translation provides translation services in 21 popular languages and 43 language directions in the world, including Chinese, English, Russian, Portuguese, Spanish, Indonesian, Thai and other popular languages, covering e-commerce shopping, daily social interaction, and overseas tourism. Relying on the leading natural language processing technology and the advantages of massive Internet data, Alibaba successfully launched the attention-based network machine translation (NMT), which allows users to tear down the language barrier, enjoy communication, and access to information.

Alibaba machine translation is a 700 million level commodity service under the group. It has built a complete set of e-commerce link solutions from multilingual station building, new business attraction, website search, user transformation to re-purchase and retention. It provides comprehensive translation services for SEO (search engine optimization), search, commodity title, commodity details (category/attributes/description), commodity review, real-time communication, audit risk control, and other e-commerce basic data, solves the basic reading needs of users in various countries for commodity related information, and provides nearly one billion level online translation services every day. Tens of thousands of QPS (queries per second) translation is done in a second. In financial year 2018, it will provide about 300 billion machine translation services for the Alibaba group.

At present, the translation tools have been also launched at Alibaba international station, which can provide real-time online translation services for suppliers in six languages. The service adopts a deep neural network machine translation system, using the latest translation framework Transformer in the industry, and a variety of artificial intelligence training methods, including domain adaptive technology, multi-model integration expert system, etc. This means that on the basis of no additional labor cost, communication efficiency can be greatly improved. A seller can understand a buyer's needs more accurately and give feedback in time. At the same time more energy is spared to improve service quality and delivery. In addition, the Alibaba international station's product details can be translated into 16 languages at the same time and synchronized to the Alibaba international station's multilingual site. Now there are more than 170 million products.

- *Time difference free inspection*

Multimedia form has taken place on the B2C e-commerce platform. In 2017 and 2016, the growth rate of Tmall's "Double 11" for multimedia broadcast reached 7600%, an explosive growth. Hubspot's consumer behavior survey also confirmed this trend: compared with only 30% of users who read graphic information, more than half (55%) of users admit they will watch the video at full length. If we want content information to be better received by users, video is the preferred media form.

The multimedia information mainly based on video is also changing the preferred way that enterprises and people get information in their daily work. According to a recent Forbes study, video information is becoming an important source of decision-making information for managers: more than 80% said they watched more online videos than a year ago; 75% viewed videos about their work on business-related websites at least weekly; and 65% visited the supplier's website for more information after watching the videos.

Cross border B2B e-commerce platform will also expand the adoption of multimedia information. For overseas buyers, multimedia information, not only video, but also more new media forms such as AR, VR, and 360 panorama, can help them understand suppliers and commodities more comprehensively and quickly, and reduce the gap caused by time and distance. The suppliers enrich the content presentation through multimedia, attract the attention of the buyers, and improve the depth and accuracy of the buyers' reception of the content. For the platform, it needs to support the whole content manufacturing chain to help suppliers quickly have the ability of multimedia marketing and adapt to this transformation. Alibaba international station has been supporting multimedia display of information since 2018, encouraging suppliers to upload content in the form of videos, moving pictures, panoramas, etc. At present, 57,000 businesses display product videos on the platform, and overseas buyers can see the product introduction in this form on the details page of more than 5.2 million kinds of products.

- *Zero distance interaction*

Also on CES in 2018, the Alibaba international station and the Electronic Devices Association of the United States jointly broadcast CES live on the Internet. In addition to the 170,000 participants attending CES who can see suppliers and exhibition commodities, tens of millions of buyers around the world can "be present" in the exhibition remotely at the same time, seeing them for the first time and interacting with the participating suppliers, communicating business opportunities, and even placing orders and trading. This attempt of online and offline linkage has covered 85 countries around the world. For the first time, cross-border B2B e-commerce has realized buying while seeing. During the live broadcast, the frequency of commodity price inquiry has been increased up to eight times. The supplier benefiting the most from live broadcast received 113 price inquiries in the four-day exhibition.

Later, the form of online exhibition will also be applied to the daily activities of the Alibaba international station, so that suppliers have more opportunities to interact with buyers from all over the world, the strength of Chinese suppliers can be shown, and business opportunities can be more efficiently seized.

*(Case source: Alibaba public information)*

### *Platform-based organizational structure*

In the DT era, "big platform + small front end" is expected to change the traditional chain-styled foreign trade and become an essential form of global business organizations, which also means the rise of platform-based organization.

Following the rapid rise of various e-commerce platforms, more and more business organizations, such as investment, employment, entrepreneurship, service, etc., develop in a platform-based direction, which closely connects a large number of global enterprises, buyers, and service providers.

The platform-based organization mode has the business organization relationship break the chain-styled multi-link model from vertical to flat:

(1) Flat transaction process. The traditional trade link begins with supply from a supplier and next there are exporters, importers, distributors at all levels, super retailers, and overseas buyers. There are many participants and links in the whole process. The "de-intermediation" effect of the Internet enables Chinese suppliers to directly face the agents and retailers at all levels behind the purchasers. Relying on the platform, buyers and sellers can complete the transaction process while conducting dynamic communication and interaction.

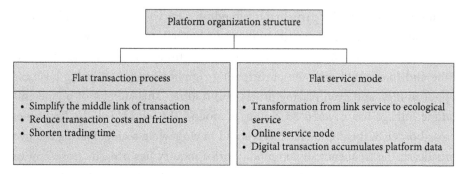

**Figure 2.10** Schematic diagram of platform-based organization structure

The flat transaction process simplifies the intermediate link, thus driving traders to strive for greater profits and buyers to get a lower price. It is able to reduce transaction cost and friction, shorten transaction time, and improve transaction efficiency and smoothness. In addition, it can enable businesses to establish efficient and dynamic supply and demand interactions with a large number of global buyers. They can directly perceive market demand and quickly innovate products, thus enriching the personalized supply of products and services and improving the overall satisfaction of foreign trade.

(2) Flat service mode. A flat platform alters the mode of foreign trade service from link service to ecological service.

In a traditional foreign trade, the intermediate links of import and export agents and offline retailers are long and redundant as a commercial chain-styled structure. And the services such as marketing, logistics, customs clearance, and post-sales are all targeted at the nodes in the chain link.

In platform-based foreign trade, the intermediate link no longer acts as an intermediary for the buyer and the seller to reach a transaction. The original offline marketing, after-sales, and other services will be online, and the logistics and payment will be the responsibility of platform-based service provider.

Although the service mode relying on the platform breaks the original chain monopoly, the flat service mode will obtain a broader online space. The massive data generated by digital exchanges will be made better use by management, analysis, market development, and product innovation with processing and analysis. At the same time, emerging value-added services such as information security, property rights protection, buyer promotion, consultation, and training will open up a broad space, bring specialized outsourcing services to the majority of SMEs and buyers and form a trading ecosystem dependent on the platform.

### Cooperation and reciprocity

In the DT era, the digital process transforms the linear supply chain system of foreign trade industry into the interconnection of the Internet. And the platform-based organization form casts great changes to the cooperation pattern.

First of all, the platform-based foreign trade organization put an end to the small-scale "human relationship" form and made it possible for large-scale collaboration and cooperative sharing of commercial and trade resources. The traditional chain-styled linear supply chain system of foreign trade, as affected by the isolation and imbalance of resources, factories and markets in time and space,

| *a* | Talent recruitment | Enterprise services | Study and progress |
|---|---|---|---|
| The average supplier service index rose from 47 to 55 | 3,000 + enterprises recruited talents | A penetration of 62,000 enterprises | 80000 foreign trade enterprises through online learning |
| 130,000 + foreign trade enterprises realize online transaction and complete transaction data accumulation | 6,000 + students got a job | The total number of orders reached 154,000 | |
| Provided financial services to 13,000 Enterprises | | | |
| Granted 16,000 loans in total | | | |
| Whose total amount reached RMB 330 million | | | |
| 36,000 enterprises adopted Cainiao Logistics | | | |
| Logistic service realizes the total visualization | In hundreds of cities and thousands of schools | Third party services | College of foreign trade |

**Figure 2.11** 2017 Alibaba international station platform services

will face a cooperation with high costs and an upper limit on the scale. So it is difficult to form large-scale cooperation.

The platform-based business pattern breaks through the edge of traditional trade cooperation and realizes the explosive integration of resources. In 2017, for example, the Alibaba international station achieved online transactions and transaction data precipitation for more than 130,000 foreign trade enterprises. In terms of finance, it provided financial services for 13,000 enterprises, with a total of 16,000 loans, totaling RMB 3.3 billion; in terms of logistics, 36,000 enterprises received Cainiao logistics services to visualize their logistics throughout the process; in terms of talent training, it helped enterprises recruit more than 3,000 talents and provide employment to 6,000 graduates through the program of "one hundred cities and one thousand schools;" in terms of enterprise ecosystem services, third party resources were hired to provide services for 62,000 enterprises, and 80,000 foreign trade enterprises gained knowledge through online learning.

Compared with these astonishing numbers, the business cooperation brought by traditional offline activities was eclipsed. The Internet breaks through the natural limitations of physical space and fully connects online and offline. The energy generated by this large-scale cooperation and sharing will far leave the traditional division of labor behind.

Secondly, large-scale business elements should be coordinated to break the low-cost competition relationship and promote the co-creation of ecosystem values with sharing, inclusiveness, and freedom as the core. The platform-based organization cuts through the traditional structure of industrial division of labor, adopts digital means to establish a network of interconnected supply chain nodes, and forms value co-creation around the needs of buyers.

The large-scale cooperation worth over RMB 100 million will inevitably lead to qualitative changes in the structure of production, trade, and consumption. The global ecosystem that circles around platforms covers B2B, B2C and C2C e-commerce forms, including trade, logistics, payment, credit investigation, credit assurance, finance, life service, and commerce. New technical elements, such as the Internet, big data, cloud computing, and artificial intelligence are involved. By integrating into the ecosystem and joining chambers of commerce and associations, enterprises share effective management experience and corporate culture, avoid vicious competition among peers, and form a new foreign trade atmosphere focusing on brand, quality, and service.

## Track of foreign trade: sweat driven, information driven to data driven

New technology gives rise to the evolution of a foreign trade business model. In this process, the trade trajectory has gone through three stages.

- *Foreign trade 1.0: sweat driven*

In traditional foreign trade, human relationships are the main way to maintain customers, while enterprises often win customers with low prices. At this time, the trade barrier was in the information asymmetry. What was production? Where were the customers? Which service providers should cooperate in the middle links? Due to the long trade chain, the search, coordination, contract signing, and operation of each link generates corresponding transaction costs.

At this stage, enterprises had to constantly be on the lookout for each other at exhibitions, understand each other in frequent cross-border exchanges, and form demand-supply relations. Therefore, foreign trade 1.0 is 100% sweat driven.

- *Foreign trade 2.0: information driven*

The advancement of Internet technology ushered foreign trade into the next stage. It enabled both parties to release supply and demand information at low cost on the Internet and complete transactions, thus overcoming the obstacles of information asymmetry and shortening the foreign trade chain.

For example, to provide online trading services to both trading sides, the Alibaba e-commerce platform was created in 1999. Platform buyers have gradually increased covering over 220 countries and regions. This third-party Internet platform enables both domestic trade and the direct selling of Chinese products abroad, so that micro-enterprises and even individuals can participate in international trade on the platform. The emergence of an international trade platform is available for developed countries, developing countries, and even poor areas in Africa. Jumia, a famous e-commerce platform in Africa, is very popular in Cameroon, Egypt, Ghana, Cote d'Ivoire, Kenya, Morocco, Nigeria, Uganda, Tanzania, and the United Kingdom.

However, despite the issue of information shortage gone, foreign trade 2.0 driven by information still fails to address the problem of energy-consuming information. In the face of massive information, enterprises find it difficult to properly make use of that. There are three shortcomings of information that need to be overcome:

(1) Information redundancy. On the Internet, information can be published at extremely low cost. The information generated in a large number of transactions and matchmaking is characterized by fragmentation and high frequency. Information needs filtering. How to effectively delete redundant information in the abundance and sift out the suitable one is costly.

(2) Information conversion. How can information be transformed into productivity in trade? In addition to reducing trade friction, it is more important to "empower" enterprises. Only the true and useful information after proper processing can be a valuable asset to productivity. For example, both sides of a transaction have to trust each other to make a deal, while the spontaneous information release on the transaction platform is difficult to provide credit support for them thousands of miles away. For another example, in international trade, the issuance of letters of credit is essential, whether the trading partners relying on the platform can prove the credit strength to the other party and the bank in the information history determines how quick the transaction can be done and financing facilitation too.

(3) Information scattering. The amount of information processed the e-commerce platform is much higher than that of agents under the traditional mode. And a transaction generates more than transaction data, but the end of the transaction, the scattered commodity logistics information, financing information, customs declaration, inspection and tax refund information. Only when all information is gathered can a complete picture of the trade be painted, so as to truly harness it for trade cost reduction.

Information flow, capital flow, and goods flow will be characterized by miniaturization, fragmentation, and high frequency in mobile Internet. If there is no efficient matching and integration of information, information driven foreign trade suffer high transaction costs regardless of the partially shortened foreign trade chain.

• *Foreign trade 3.0: data driven*

Swamped by massive information, the direction of foreign trade development in the future is characterized by accurate matching. Data-driven foreign trade 3.0 can fully overcome the information shortcomings of foreign trade 2.0. "Data empowerment" is achievable with the participation of huge amount of supply and demand data and the adoption of big data.

With the generation and application of cloud storage and big data, the massive, scattered, idle, and abundant data resources can be made use of, therefore achieving the transformation of foreign trade from sweat driven to data driven. This kind of drive not only lowers the human cost of constantly hunting for customers, but also empowers businesses with credit.

---

**CASE STUDIES**   Data driven at the Alibaba International station

In DT era, the Alibaba international station is becoming a digital trade infrastructure platform.

At the front end, the Alibaba international station provides one-hour inquiry reply and online real-time translation for cross-border e-commerce sellers who are not familiar with foreign language services. This reduces the communication costs and trust costs between the buyer and the seller and improves the inquiry conversion rate; regarding non-face-to-face customer trust issues, credit system construction and credit disclosure services reduce the credit cost for both sides.

In the middle stage, the international station improves the accuracy of matching between the buyer and the seller by layering the seller and seals the transaction faster. The credit assurance products solve the performance guarantee problem in the whole transaction process; both sides can also obtain the credit sales and supply chain loans made by the international station through the accumulated credit.

At the rear end, Alibaba launched OneTouch to solve the problem of slow customs clearance, difficult tax refunds, and high costs of foreign exchange settlement for most SMEs. It enables each link of customs to be completed in an hour. The single window mode of OneTouch can complete export by gathering orders. It successfully solves the problem that SMEs used to look for one-to-one single point service providers when they carried out international trade. In addition, OneTouch will join hands with Cainiao logistics to help small- and medium-sized sellers to consolidate the bulk orders. The combination of orders makes it possible for small sellers' goods to be shipped by ships and airplanes, the logistics services and prices that were only available to international giants.

\* \* \*

## Transformation confusion in the new trend

In continuous technological change, foreign trade enterprises have three choices of foreign trade modes: maintaining the traditional offline foreign trade, i.e. foreign trade 1.0; relying on the online foreign trade e-commerce platform to embark on foreign trade 2.0; and participating in the global trade ecology 3.0 driven by data. In fact, most of the domestic foreign trade enterprises, including processing enterprises and trade enterprises, still stay in the first stage, far behind the requirements of the DT era in concept, technology, and mode.

The impact of new technology will change the foreign trade mode. And the traditional foreign trade will face a more difficult situation and inevitably transform.

### *Poor, no more traditional advantageous cost*

After the rapid development of foreign trade exports since China's accession to the WTO, the traditional dividend period of China's foreign trade has gradually disappeared. External exports have been in a recession while the costs of internal raw materials and human resources have been rising. As a result, the advantageous cost no longer exists. And it requires more efforts to obtain orders.

On the one hand, the comparative advantage of production cost no longer exists. According to BCG's economic analysis report on global manufacturing migration, since the 21st century, wages in the top 25 export manufacturing countries have generally increased. Contrary to other economies whose annual wage growth rate was only 2%–3%, that in China was as high as 10%–20%. In terms of energy, the cost of electricity and gas in China has risen by nearly 70% and 140% in the past decade. China has lost its low-cost advantage.

On the other hand, in the context of industrial transformation and upgrading, the advantages of China's land and foreign capital preferential policies have gradually reduced or weakened. Compared with Southeast Asian countries and India, Chinese enterprise no longer have advantageous prices. Inevitably, processing and manufacturing orders continue to flow to countries with lower cost.

The transformation is no piece of cake. Facing the transformation from the seller's market to the buyer's market, the advantages of empiricism and effective channels are no longer working but have become dusty history. The traditional competitive advantage of China's foreign trade is weakening, the new competitive advantage has not yet formed, and the industrial development is facing the dual pressure from both developed countries and other developing countries. Enterprises embracing traditional foreign trade have to power through the pressure of operation in the new situation. Transformation and upgrading are both necessary and urgent.

### Weak, low-end's difficulty to change

In traditional foreign trade enterprises, OEM (Original Equipment Manufacturer) and ODM (Original Design Manufacturer) are very common. OEM and ODM are often difficult to really hold the pricing power of products. Price competition and small profits yet high sales have become the competitive strategies of many enterprises. Under the background of global industrial transfer, traditional foreign trade enterprises suffer the dilemma that cost advantage no longer exists and the dilemma that price is forced to be lowered in the intensified market competition. The profits are getting increasingly worse.

In OEM and ODM, although the enterprise has the same or similar design and production capacity as the famous brand, it is still locked in the low-end links such as production, processing, assembly, etc., where product added value is low. The lack of an independent brand makes it difficult for an industrial transformation and upgrading, hence the dilemma of being stuck at low-end.

It can be explained both internally and externally.

First, enterprises' more attention to a single link in offline trade leaves them dependent with a weak sense of transformation and development. The growth of China's foreign trade enterprises benefits from the institutional changes of China's reform and opening up and the huge dividends brought by the last round of globalization. The long-term focus on offline trading in a single link makes the enterprises lack of enough attention to marketing, branding, and patents. They do not have such great motivation, ability, and courage to change the situation of being stuck at low-end. Even if there is external technology impact, they are difficult to adapt themselves to independent innovation.

Second, multinational companies with the leading position in the value chain lift the threshold of enterprise transformation by setting up barriers to knowledge innovation and technical standards and blocking technology and marketing channels. This weakens the transformation and development ability of traditional foreign trade enterprises. As the say in traditional trade is controlled by large multinational companies, it is difficult for Chinese traditional trade enterprises, which struggle at daily operations, to change their thinking. Moreover, it is expensive to change the low-end situation via innovation.

A journey of a thousand miles begins with a single step. However, when foreign trade enterprises take the first step of transformation, all kinds of confusion come one after another, of which the first is the target confusion. The first step of enterprise transformation is to define the market positioning, which determines the direction, layout, and input of corresponding resources of its development. Where is the target customer? What is the enterprise positioning? How to maintain continuous innovation? This is what the traditional export-oriented enterprises lack in OEM mode and what the traditional foreign trade agencies are confused about.

### Blocked, long chains leading to weak operation

In traditional foreign trade activities, many small- and medium-sized foreign trade enterprises have not been granted the permission to engage in import and export because there is administrative approval which determines the right to export tax rebate and the right to import and export. Consequently, foreign trade agents have become an indispensable part of many links. These agents profit from the advantage of low input price and information asymmetry. The situation is characterized by separation of production and sales, which is an important reason for China's foreign trade ecological fragility.

*Commodity circulation is blocked.* Agents, often in the possession of light assets, are more flexible in operation. When the macro-economy and foreign trade situation change, a large number of foreign trade intermediaries will be forced to change business or even go bankrupt. Their elimination breaks the long chain of foreign trade, blocks the commodity channel from the manufacturer to the buyer, causes a chain reaction, and then results in the export-oriented manufacturing enterprises' bankruptcy. The ultimate outcome is the decline of foreign trade imports and exports.

*Product innovation is blocked.* In the long chain of foreign trade, the existence of agents has become a barrier for communication between manufacturers and buyers. Export-oriented manufacturers lack of direct interaction with buyers for a long time, thus unable to grasp the first-hand market demand in time, and the upgrading and innovation of products seriously lag behind.

For a long time, foreign trade enterprises have experienced a blocking of commodity circulation and product innovation. They have difficulties in adapting to the operation characteristics of the Internet and DT era in terms of operation management, talent gathering, and service upgrading.

*Operation confusion.* Transformation means a change of thinking patterns. On the one hand, traditional foreign trade enterprises will have a significant change in operation mode from facing foreign trade dealers to consumers directly; on the other hand, they will move business from offline to online, which is completely different. How to take advantage of the platform to operate? How to design product pages? How to better realize the effective promotion of commodities and channels? The business model of foreign trade enterprises will undergo colossal changes.

*Talent confusion.* When traditional foreign trade enterprises transform to foreign trade 3.0, teams with experience in e-commerce and big data operation are needed to take charge of operation and management. How to recruit or cultivate talents with such experience? How to coordinate with traditional procurement and production departments? How to integrate traditional foreign trade with new technology? These are all problems that foreign trade enterprises must tackle in the process of transformation.

*Service confusion.* In foreign trade 3.0, foreign trade enterprises have to confront the overseas market directly. This means more difficulties for traditional enterprises. Enterprises must become more familiar with overseas policies and regulations, cultural customs. They have to grasp consumer preferences more directly and quickly and use local languages more fluently. How to arrange market follow-up service overseas? How to make use of the platform to get better related services? These are the necessary conditions for the successful transformation of enterprises.

Facing the unstoppable trend of cross-border e-commerce, more and more traditional foreign trade enterprises have become aware of the transformation of e-commerce. However, how can they survive the change of market morphology? How to adapt to changes in buyer demand and transaction mode? What is the direction of transformation? These difficulties and confusions come with both opportunities and challenges for traditional foreign trade enterprises.

# CHAPTER III

# Big Data's Reconstruction of New Foreign Trade

A T PRESENT, CHINA IS actively blending in globalization. President Xi Jinping pointed out at the Boao Forum for Asia April 2018 that "China's economic development had been achieved under open conditions in the past 40 years and its future high-quality development must also be carried out under more open terms." Meanwhile, it should be noted that since the 21st century began, the global digital economy has bloomed. The number of global netizens has exceeded four billion at the beginning of 2018. More than half of the world's population embraces the Internet. In the era of the digital economy, global trade is within the reach of everyone.

Of the 40 million SMEs in China, three to five million are focused on foreign trade, which contributed to 60% of the import and export volume.[1] In most countries, SMEs are the main body of the economy. In the new trade era of "global buying and selling," an increasing number of them from various countries will join the global trade through cross-border e-commerce. So, how can they become active participants in international trade by means of e-commerce? Is it possible to enter the global value chain and international market with the help of new technology or even stand on the same starting line as large enterprises through "little strength?"

---

1. Source: National Bureau of statistics

*   *   *

# New foreign trade, new journey

## *Opportunities in changes*

All the transformation of foreign trade is built on the change of trade itself and the change of customer demand. Today, foreign trade has gone through sweat-driven foreign trade 1.0 and stepped into the later stage of information-driven foreign trade 2.0. Regarding the changing trends and environment, the elephant in the room for enterprises is that as difficulty has increased to run a business, they are put at the crossroad of transformation.

To find the key to the transformation, the difficulties must be understood. They come in three aspects: difficulty in landing an order, in financing, and in circulation.

First, it is difficult to obtain an order. Later in the information-driven stage, the unavailability of flow dividend sets more obstacles to land orders.

In the second chapter, three stages of foreign trade: sweat-driven, information-driven and data-driven are discussed. In these three stages, the core competitiveness of foreign trade has gradually changed. The first stage depends on the ability of foreign trade salesman, including the level of receiving orders and the ability of transforming an inquiry into an order; the second stage relies on the ability of e-commerce operation and platform skills. But in the trend of more prevalent platform and the Internet, a large number of business has been transferred from offline to online, ergo leaving information growingly transparent. The price is more transparent and the flow dividend is gone. Therefore, it can be found that the cost of relying on online platforms to find customers and buyers will continue to grow. Many enterprises regard the network platform as the main export channel, but it is more difficult to obtain orders.

Second, financing is challenging. In the information-driven stage, we notice that many foreign trade enterprises begin to use Internet tools and take the network platform as the main export channel. At this stage, SMEs have equal access to information, except still unequal access to resources, an essential one of which in a transaction is capital. The difficulty of financing is still a high threshold for SMEs to participate in foreign trade.

The common experience of foreign trade enterprises is that banks find it difficult to open financing channels to SMEs or the channels are very limited and their cost is still high. For example, letter of credit or credit sale prevails in foreign trade except that SMEs are difficult to obtain the relevant services of banks due to their limited assets and credit. Capital constraints have greatly limited the development speed of SMEs. Even if they land high-quality buyers and orders, it is difficult to cash in the orders but miss them.

> **CASE STUDIES**  Common problems of financing difficulty in cross-border transactions of SMEs

There is asymmetric credit information between the two sides of cross-border transactions, especially for small- and medium-sized participants. The credit status of the counterparty is not only one of the most concerning factors, but also one of the most difficult to judge and obtain information about. Owing to the lack of credit information, it is challenging for the common financing approaches in traditional international trade to apply, which leads to the financing dilemma.

- Difficult for letter of credit to apply. The letter of credit is widely used in international trade. However, small- and medium-sized enterprise customers are often faced with three practical problems when they take orders on letter of credit. First, the operation of the letter of credit is too complex to be understood and performed by ordinary foreign traders; second, the letter of credit itself has the risks of inconsistency and the joint fraud by overseas buyers and the issuing bank; third, they shoulder the pressure of goods preparation and production funds in letter of credit orders after acceptance.
- Credit sales are highly risky. A credit sale is a very common way for buyers in developed countries such as Europe and the United States. It is also widely used in China's foreign trade exports. When small- and medium-sized customers receive credit sales orders, two fundamental problems require immediate solution: one is how to ensure that suppliers can receive payment from purchasers when they deliver goods as promised; the other is the capital pressure of production/stock during the execution of credit sales orders.
- Mixed feelings for the accounting period. In B2B offline transactions, the accounting period is a very common and widely accepted way of transaction by SMEs. There are several difficulties in the account period transaction that give SMEs mixed feelings: for buyers, it does not occupy funds, but at the same time, the selection range of merchants will be limited and the quota of the

accounting period is not enough in the peak of purchase season; for sellers (suppliers), it is very helpful to maintain the old business relationship, but the risk of non-payment and the funds occupying turnover has always been a headache.

Third, circulation is difficult. Information drive can accelerate the efficiency of foreign trade matching, but it still cannot change the nature as a long chain; the follow-up process of foreign trade must rely on offline services, which makes difficult circulation an unsolvable problem stage 2.0.

Obviously, foreign trade 2.0 is gradually becoming the past. Foreign trade 3.0 will start from solving these three difficulties and gradually become a new trend as the new foreign trade.

As the new era approaches, the changes of trade mode, main body, patterns, and rules indicate that cross-border trade will embrace a new form.

What is new foreign trade? We should start with its two features.

The most distinctive feature of new foreign trade is the ability of data application. After foreign trade 2.0 and online trading, data resources are applied to the whole trading closed-loop and data closed-loop through data precipitation. The application of emerging technologies in e-commerce platform enables the trading parties to break the distance of time, space, and culture, and communicate more closely and efficiently; the trading parties can search information online while completing a series of work such as payment, logistics, customs clearance, etc. through an e-commerce platform and can stay posted on the order progress in real time; the platform builds a credit system to better match supply and demand and optimize services by accumulating identity information, behavioral patterns, and capabilities of both parties. The data of foreign trade transaction and circulation are continuously deposited and utilized for the reconstruction of

**Figure 3.1** Two features of new foreign trade

each circulation link of the trade order. Through reconstruction, cost is reduced, precise transaction is realized, and new foreign trade is completed.

The other feature is the ecological value chain. While ecosystem resources are used to generate value and partners of different environments around serve you and help improve efficiency, you also become a part of their value, co-creating value and reducing cost. The interconnection of the global trade network is the ultimate goal of the new foreign trade transformation. The mode of China's cross-border trade e-commerce platform and comprehensive services is replicated to other countries to provide markets, platforms, and capabilities for small- and medium-sized foreign trade enterprises of all countries, forming a "global buying and selling" trade network ecology.

So, how does new foreign trade use data and ecological value chain to solve three new problems: difficulty in landing an order, financing, and circulation?

On the first level, the closed loop of data breaks the difficulty in landing an order.

After the enterprise relies on the platform to accumulate and continuously deposit the data of transaction, logistics, and other links, these data can be fed back to each link of the transaction, forming new business opportunities, which is the closed loop of data.

In the entire closed loop of data, when data is fed back to the information level, it will bring more business opportunities; when it is fed back to the transaction level, it will bring credit assurance, thus ensuring the transaction safety of both parties, so that they can quickly reach a transaction with reduced communication costs; when it is fed back to the service link, it can provide comprehensive foreign trade services by relying on data and platforms to help enterprises settle foreign exchange, pass customs and refund tax to reduce costs; when it is fed back to the logistics link, lower discount logistics services can be accessed, even a small amount of logistics services; when it is fed back to the financial link, credit financial services can be accessed such as flow loans and online business loans.

Today, data begins to flow in the whole foreign trade transaction chain, and is gradually fed back to each link, forming a huge amount of data application value.

On the second level, digital credit solves financing problems.

Transaction data, as the basic data of enterprises, can well measure the credit status of enterprises. The establishment of an effective credit system is the core of the prosperity of the financial industry, and also the key to accessing to financial services. The use of these data can help small- and medium-sized foreign trade

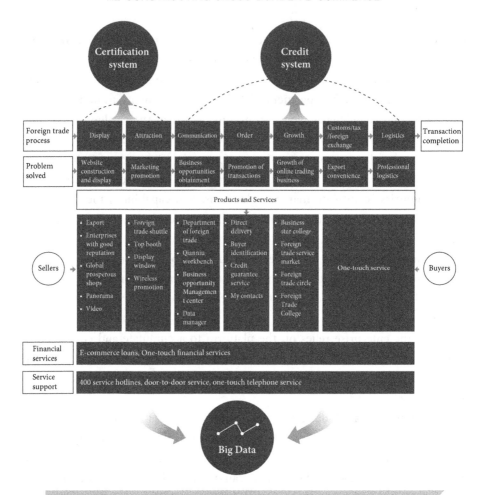

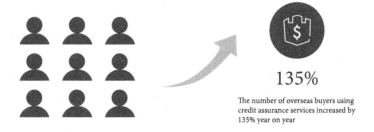

**Figure 3.2** Alibaba digital closed-loop service

*Source: Alibaba public information*

enterprises get the best orders efficiently, access to financial services at a low cost, and obtain commercial credit at the initial stage of enterprise establishment.

Low cost credit. Based on the data accumulated by the platform, small loans, online business loans or flow loans can be made. The platform can allocate a certain proportion of loans correspondingly to the amount of deposits the enterprise makes while selling on credit to overseas buyers. Behind the data is more than how many orders the platform can bring, but also how much credit capabilities and credit sales capabilities the enterprises have today. The ultimate result is improvement of the enterprise's ability to receive orders.

Survival of the fittest industry. Enterprises with excellent products and good reputations can easily obtain the support of credit assurance, credit loans, and other financial services while avoiding the adverse situation of Gresham's law in the financial field. And good enterprises can enjoy financial services and thrive.

In credit-driven transactions, buyers can quickly locate the proper seller with the help of this data. Financial institutions can also make decisions efficiently and develop supply chain finance. Thanks to big data, the transaction credit and capital problems that have troubled many SMEs have been solved.

Third, ecological value chain services put an end to difficulty in circulation.

Compared with other transactions, the export procedures of foreign trade are much more complex. Online operation is difficult for some traditional foreign trade enterprises. Many foreign trade enterprises are not only not professional enough for online operations, but also are still in a difficult position to implement many processes.

However, after the growth of foreign trade 2.0, there are many service providers and channel providers around the B2B platform today to help enterprises provide professional services. When a shop has no idea on decoration, a professional shop decoration service provider is ready to help; when there is lack of talent, third party companies recruit talents on their behalf; when operation is stuck, independent operating companies can work for them. Some enterprises have strong R & D and production capacity, but they are not unqualified or even incapable at sales. At this time, a new combination of production and sales can be made, thus making up for the shortcomings of the enterprise and forming a new one as a whole without shortcoming by cooperation with marketing and foreign trade agencies.

In addition to providing services based on the demands of enterprises, the chamber of commerce, lecturer system, and various sharing meetings in the ecosystem also undertake the functions of sharing excellent management mode and employee incentive mode and incubating new foreign trade enterprises.

With the help from the professional services of the ecosystem, the circulation difficulty that foreign trade enterprises are confronted with have been solved. And a more convenient and efficient closed loop of foreign trade circulation has gradually come into being.

### Co-create value

This ecosystem model of new foreign trade conforms to the concept of sharing the economy in the Internet era. The massive, scattered, idle, and surplus resources, such as space, capital, professional knowledge, and skills, are fully made use of. And the utilization efficiency of resources is improved.

As there is a large number of independent professional divisions of the platform, each enterprise has a unique professional team to serve. And for each specific business, one or more service types are available in the ecosystem to provide business support. These ecosphere professional organizations continue to provide services for enterprises while foreign trade enterprises act as their survival partners in return. This is a process of mutual service and completion and of value co-creation, which is the very core of the foreign trade ecosystem.

\* \* \*

# New foreign trade enabling enterprises

The new era of foreign trade is around the corner. The e-commerce platform that relies on new technology innovation harnesses big data and comprehensive trade services to enable information exchange, service sharing, and credit transparency in cross-border trade. As a result, a "global buying and selling" trade ecosystem is formed. And SMEs are continuously enabled to thrive.

### Approaching transformation

New foreign trade supplies the Internet infrastructure and lowers the transformation bar of foreign trade enterprises. The transformation is difficult, because on the one hand it takes time to master the thinking pattern of foreign trade 3.0. More importantly, it needs corresponding infrastructure, such as information supporting of space, transportation, plants, and storage. Meanwhile, it is also necessary to better understand the legal system, culture, credit, and other soft power. The new foreign trade platform virtualizes the physical infrastructure and moves it to the Internet, which greatly reduces the basic investment required by the information transformation of foreign trade enterprises. And the virtual facilities such as the legal system, culture, and credit can be internalized in the foreign trade platform itself, thus lowing the bar for foreign trade enterprises to transform. The investment of foreign trade facilities in the new foreign trade is about 30% lower than that in the traditional foreign trade.

New foreign trade provides a specialized package of services to reduce the transformation cost of foreign trade enterprises. It links up orders, logistics, and capital of foreign trade transactions, forms a unified platform, and provides specialized services by creating an ecosystem there. These services are committed to reducing the various costs of traders in each link. These costs include that of searching supply and demand, of matching supply and demand, of negotiations, of credit, of customs clearance, and of logistics, and even of financing and data at a higher level. Therefore, a complete and low-cost transaction chain integrating information flow, capital flow, and logistics comes into being. New foreign trade reduces transaction costs and requires a lower transformation cost for foreign trade enterprises by improving transaction efficiency.

Alibaba's new foreign trade can more easily push forward the transformation and development of foreign trade enterprises. An entrepreneur without online foreign trade experience can also adapt to the development trend of foreign trade 3.0 by understanding Alibaba's foreign trade platform. Interviews and questionnaire surveys reveal the operating cost of foreign trade enterprises on Alibaba foreign trade platform is on average 30% less than offline operations, the average proportion of order increase is 76%, that of profit increase is 32%, and the annual profit increase is about RMB 400,000.

## *Trade Expressway*

The new foreign trade model tears down the credit barrier between the buyer and the seller, the foreign trade provider, and the service provider with Internet big data so as to enable a smooth foreign trade process.

New foreign trade tears down the barriers of trust and accelerates the obtainment of trade orders. In traditional trade, it is difficult for buyers and sellers to understand each other's trade history and trade credit at a low cost. Trade enterprises need to show their corporate credit by decorating stores, building brands, and even founding large and multinational companies. Relying on Internet information participation and the harnessing of big data information, new foreign trade enables the traceability and query of transaction histories and buyer's evaluations, thus making it possible for the low-cost display of buyer's credit and forming credit information for more effective and rapid use. Buyers can quickly identify the required sellers in the data and seal the deal at a faster rate.

New foreign trade tears down the financing barriers and promotes the financing in trade. One of the core problems that challenge a large number of small- and medium-sized foreign trade enterprises in the process of innovation and development is the financing difficulties. It is common that those that have already received the order cannot complete it due to the shortage of funds. In fact, the core of the financing difficulties of SMEs lies in that under the current system, commercial banks cannot accurately and cheaply conduct credit investigations on them, therefore are unable to grant financial services. In the new foreign trade mode, the e-commerce platform can accurately check the credit of enterprises at low cost by the participation and analysis of transaction data. As a result, the financing problem is gone.

New foreign trade tears down the service barriers in the industrial chain of foreign trade and improves the overall transaction efficiency. In reality, it is difficult for foreign trade enterprises to engage in production, sales, logistics, and service at the same time. For example, in September 2017, the Alibaba international station fully opened the order flow and logistics to escort online cross-border trade orders. Up to now, the order quantity of logistics order (express delivery) has increased fivefold. The Alibaba international station in 2018 launched a Sino-US special line that guarantees delivery within 5 days, a 24-hour service response mechanism, and zero delays at peak season service. At the same time, the online visual tracking of logistics takes effect, so that enterprises joining the platform can "do light" as much as possible. The new foreign trade mode reduces the transaction cost and lowers the transaction bar generally by tearing down the service barriers in the industrial chain of foreign trade. This effectively improves the transaction efficiency, and further the business value of both parties.

**CASE STUDIES** Alibaba credit data assists SMEs to operate in foreign trade

Alibaba.com's credit assurance service vouches for suppliers with good credit on the platform, while provide financing services for SMEs to improve their international competitiveness. Through this service, the supplier can obtain a credit assurance line of up to US$1 million. At present, the service has granted more than 150,000 Alibaba.com members credit lines, with a sum of more than US$7 billion. In 2017, there were 61,000 suppliers receiving the services, an increase of 45% over 2016.

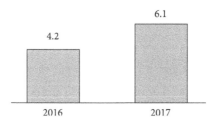

**Figure 3.3** Alibaba's number of suppliers using credit assurance (unit: 10,000)

## Instant access to the market

New foreign trade broadens the channel market and the number of transactions increases in geometric progression. The Alibaba international station, as an information and trading platform, provides conditions for the transaction, allowing it to be made at any time and place, an absolute advantage over traditional foreign trade. And as a sufficient number of supply and demand parties stay on the platform, the use of big data is conducive to accurately matching supply and demand and facilitating transactions. The new foreign trade platform has greatly improved the transaction efficiency, allowing the number of transactions to increase in geometric progression. Taking Alibaba.com as an example, the growth of online trading orders and amount was stable in 2017. Especially at the end of that year, the trading volume and amount surged two-three times compared with the same period in 2016.

New foreign trade extends an enterprise's reach and improves their innovative thinking and efficiency. Foreign trade enterprises can depend on the Alibaba foreign trade platform to expand their range directly to foreign wholesalers and

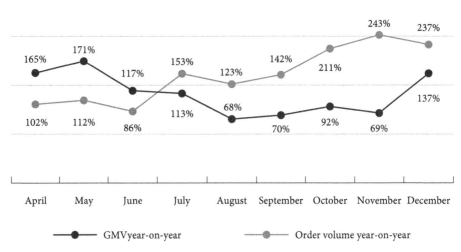

**Figure 3.4** Growth of Alibaba credit assurance GMV and order volume from April to December 2017

even consumers, which was unimaginable under the traditional foreign trade mode. The advantage of the extension to the terminal is that it can greatly propel enterprises to grasp the demand party's preferences and changes of the market situation as well as optimize the experience of the demand party's customers. At the same time, the Alibaba foreign trade platform has altered the perspective of foreign trade enterprises from the original middleman information to the global transparent information, which has greatly enlarged an enterprise's reach.

New foreign trade alters thinking patterns and helps enterprises achieve "fine business and fine products." First, the construction of a foreign trade business ecosystem gives rise to a mutually beneficial and shared foreign trade ecosystem. The participating foreign trade enterprises gradually get rid of the business culture of vicious price competition and take sharing and co-operation as the deep idea of enhancing enterprise value instead. Second, with the help of platform and information technology, new foreign trade provides enterprises with personalized business matching and financial services by feeding back data, analysis, and exploration to them. In the process of these services, it drives them to complete the structural reform concerning the supply side and provide more "fine business and fine product" that meet the needs of buyers, which is conducive to the overall improvement of China's foreign trade quality.

Alibaba OneTouch ecological service

The Alibaba B2B foreign trade comprehensive service department (OneTouch) officially launched "One Partner," which introduces various localized foreign trade service enterprises (such as freight forwarders, import and export agents, customs brokers, finance and taxation companies, etc.) as partners to provide more complete localization, personal, and personalized low-cost comprehensive services focused on exports for foreign trade enterprises, especially SMEs. Targeting the fragmented and individualized needs of enterprises clients, it makes one-stop solution available. "One partner" enterprises provide agency services in a self-operating mode, including providing customers with consulting services related to OneTouch export customs clearance, foreign exchange settlements, tax refunds, finance, and logistics as well as foreign trade services such as order formulation, order placement, and order tracking. Meanwhile, partners can customize logistics and guide the handling of commodity inspection according to their own business advantages throughout the process to provide customers with more complete foreign trade services. "One partner" enables foreign trade services to be implemented and upgraded by aggregating resource systems and establishes an offline ecosystem of foreign trade services.

\* \* \*

## Supplier portrait 3.0

*Business opportunity of data*

In the future, data utilization will be an important business opportunity for foreign trade enterprises.

For a long time, the difficulty of winning customers is often the common situation for SMEs. They search on the Internet, participate in activities, and release information or ask for recommendations. These are often inefficient and instable. And the promotion costs of many mainstream paid channels are also climbing year by year, which makes marketing increasingly difficult. New foreign trade, with the help of the e-commerce platform and big data, uses and applies data while establishing credit files for enterprises, which gradually evolves into a kind of service for them to explore more business opportunities.

Relying on big data, the analysis of the multi-dimensional information of the target enterprise, such as the region, industry, business scope, main products, company scale, organizational structure, etc. helps enterprises to screen similar customer leads in the massive amount of data. Assistance is given to SMEs to insight into customers as well as clear business guidance, and ultimately to improve their ability to get customers.

In addition to that, data can also improve enterprises' acquisition capacity of effective customers. Big data analysis can identify the risk of common fraud, control the quality of customers, reduce the bad debt rate, enhance the screening ability of effective customers, and locate efficient customers.

In the Christmas of 2017, big data recommended Chinese enterprises to American customers by analyzing the demand of American buyers for Christmas hats (such as size, style, etc.) individually. A customer in the U.S. tried to make a purchase online on the platform. To his surprise, the Christmas hat from China was delivered three hours later and the transaction complete. Why was it so fast? Because big data already understands the needs of overseas buyers on Christmas Eve. The Chinese company has stored goods in the U.S. warehouse for Christmas in advance.

Compared with the traditional three-month maritime logistics or three-week cross-border logistics, the three-hour delivery experience greatly improves customer satisfaction with suppliers. Consumption demand outlined by big data helps enterprises better obtain orders. An American buyer, via big data matching, only needs one click on the mouse to find the most suitable Chinese seller. In the past, the buyer needed at least eight links to finally purchase Christmas hats from a factory in the Luohu District of Shenzhen. Big data matching lifted the efficiency of sales by 300%–400%.

---

**CASE STUDIES**   "Big 3C" business opportunity of data

---

The Big 3C industry (computing, communications, and consumable electronic devices) is one of the four industry categories on which the Alibaba international station industry operation focuses. The Alibaba international station, with trendy new and cost-effective products, meets 3C buyers' one-stop efficient procurement needs.

- Buyer's mind. The turnover of goods is fast, and the buyer's demand for new products is obvious, including new product trends, quality requirements, inventory assurance, visual logistics, after-sales service, etc. For this reason, Alibaba applies the strategy of a focus on new products and efficient procurement.
- Selection of new products for efficient sourcing. It strives to provide product testing videos, shorten the purchase hesitation period and communication, build rich 3C trading scenarios, select new fine 3C products, and gather orders.
- Online trading of specifications. It strives to establish an online transaction of specification products, that is, establish 3C buyer's purchase records and purchase relationship, linkage with merchant's preference, one-click return, etc.
- Setup of efficient delivery mechanism. It strives to cooperate with the third party's overseas storage, assist the overseas local merchants to quickly deliver goods, and set up a sample area to improve the buyer's shopping experience.

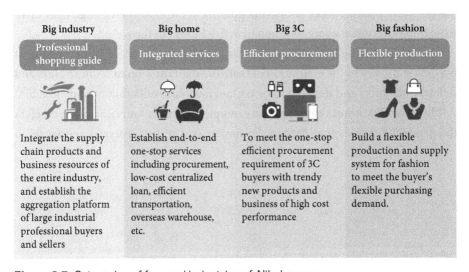

**Figure 3.5** Categories of focused industries of Alibaba.com

### Flexible supply

The new foreign trade will change both the sales mode and the supply mode, i.e. new manufacturing.

The flexible supply mode of new manufacturing includes two driving force chains. First, in the context of consumption upgrading, the market demand of international consumers tends to be personalized, especially the younger generation of consumers are more in pursuit of unique goods. Consumers often have faster, better, and more personalized requirements for goods, which will drive the supply party to continuously meet consumer demand by customization, mixed innovation, and flexible production. Second, the change of demand in the terminal market is gradually reflected in its upstream supply roles. Retailers will heed more to the diversity and uniqueness of products and the possibility of rapid market entry when purchasing, thus requiring small orders, short cycles, and fast delivery. For suppliers, small orders also mean lower risk, faster capital turnover, and generally higher profits.

Alibaba.com data shows that compared with distributors, factories, and import and export companies, smaller retailers account for an increasing proportion of buyers year by year. In 2014, retailers accounted for less than 25% of the active buyers of the website, while as of the beginning of 2018, the percentage went up to 34%. It has become the largest group of active buyers of the website.

Fragmentation of foreign trade orders has become a trend. The harnessing of big data is the key to the realization of that. The digitalization of online buyers and sellers, trade links and demand information, flexible production is made feasible.

Take the Christmas shopping as an example. When an American buyer receives the goods, he notices that despite the similar cost of this material and fabric to

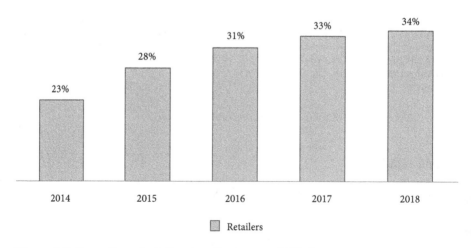

**Figure 3.6** Proportion of retailers in active buyers of Alibaba.com

that of the previous purchase, they sell better than he expects. This is because big data analyzes the demand of American consumers in advance. So he wants to replenish by placing the second order. He would like one-third of the order to be embroidered with a personalized logo and two-thirds to be decorated with wigs. The information can be quickly fed back via the Internet platform. Chinese platform traders rely on the ecological chain partners to quickly complete the production of small orders. Flexible production and small-order customization can make sure styles and patterns are in line with the personalized needs of customers. A hat used to be priced US$14, and flexible customization increased the value of the product to US$20.

Big-data flexible supply brings customers to the enterprise as well as improves its profit margin and product added value.

---

**CASE STUDIES** "Big fashion" flexible supply

The "big fashion" industry is one of the four industries that Alibaba international station industry operation focuses on. The international station builds a flexible production and supply system of fashion in combination with "fine business" to meet the flexible purchasing demands of buyers.

- Buyer's mind: online retailers are the main body with purchase of high-frequency, order of fragmentation, and requirement of sample trial order; small order customization demand is popular and the buyer pays attention to seasonal and trend products, the quantity of standard products is large, and the demand stable.
- Business insight: the U.S. is still a major exporting destination while Southeast Asia and the Middle East are opportunities for the apparel industry. In terms of domestic supply, key industries are concentrated, such as Qingdao wigs and Guangzhou clothing, while fast fashion consumer categories are looking for opportunities for fast proofing. Therefore, Alibaba implements the leading strategy of "fast proofing service, processing customization scenarios."
- Fast proofing service. The focus is on the apparel industry and a fixed price for the sample. With the Chinese Taobao brand combined with express logistics, fast proofing services are made available. The infrastructure of online transactions is improved, a variety of marketing scenarios are built, the purchasing relationship bridged, and orders returned with one click.

- Business pool service of flexible supply chain. Suppliers with proofing, micro design, integrated procurement, and rapid response capabilities are mined and cultivated, and flow equity mechanism established.
- Processing customization scenarios. Demand is aggregated, creating vertical scenes of the processing customization industry and accurate flow matching, and opening up supply chain services.

### Cloud supply chain

Supply chain is a whole functional network chain, which involves suppliers, manufacturers, distributors, retailers, and end users in the process of purchasing raw materials, manufacturing and processing, and delivering finished products to consumers. For foreign trade enterprises, a new supply chains extend beyond the traditional one to customs clearance, foreign exchange settlements, tax refunds, insurance, finance, and logistics as the longest process chain.

Small enterprises usually start to build a supply chain in the third year of operation. The supply chain business involves many participants, including enterprises, logistics providers, customs, and final consumers. The connection is no piece of cake. Today's Internet will alter the mainstream value of manufacturing enterprises. It is no longer the online business based on traffic logic in the past, but the connection of all value links of the industrial chain with the help of platforms and big data. Internet enterprises represented by Alibaba strive to build a supply chain infrastructure, while a cloud-based supply chain can connect these decentralized systems and data sources in a unified way, form effective information sharing, and zero delay communication among all parties, and promote collaborative work. The information system, big data, and cloud computing together give rise to a cloud supply chain.

Free inspection service is an example of the cloud supply chain. The Alibaba international station made free inspection services available to the buyer during the purchasing festival in September 2017. The buyer who chooses the inspection service can contact the inspection service provider through the platform to conduct the inspection. During the whole procurement period, a total of 17,000 orders were qualified for free inspection.

Foreign trade enterprises can directly make use of these cloud infrastructures, such as the cloud supply chain, to realize the seamless connection of various links in the whole life cycle of foreign trade, such as cloud credit, cloud logistics, cloud transactions, cloud payments, etc. They can even carry out the supply chain process tracing and resource sharing on the basis of the connection and optimize the decision-making with big data analysis to improve the overall efficiency and experience of the supply chain. When the foreign trade platform reduces the business costs and simplifies the business process by the large-scale processing, enterprises can get rid of the business process by subcontracting the enterprise functions such as sales, customs clearance, and tax refunds to the platform.

The inspection service of the cloud supply chain contributed to the 64% of the payment conversion rate of the enterprise's order higher than that without inspection service. As a regular service option on Alibaba international, buyers and sellers can choose directly according to their own needs in daily trading scenarios and cloud infrastructure will effectively help seal deals.

**CASE STUDIES** "Big home" cloud supply chain

The "big home" industry is one of the four industries that the Alibaba international station industry operation focuses on. The international station establishes "end-to-end" one-stop services such as procurement, low-cost goods collection, efficient transportation, overseas warehouses, etc. in combination with the cloud supply chain.

- Buyers' mind: the buyer of furniture and lamps is accustomed to trial purchases and has high requirements for the service of the supplier, including product innovation, quality assurance, and stable supply. Most of the products are light or heavy goods, which are mainly transported by sea. There is a great demand for inspection and logistics services.
- Business insight: there are many home furnishing industry clusters in China, which are the representatives of China's advantageous manufacturing industry, which targets the United States as the main market of large home furnishings. There are great demands for export order guarantees and sea freight LCL. And pre-inspection and shipping LCL service link online transaction. For this reason, Alibaba implements the leading strategy of "service upgrading, viscosity improvement, and re-purchase."

(1) It can meet the buyer's rigid demand for inspection, provide inspection services, and improve the buyer's repurchase and data participation.

(2) LCL service, embedded in the online order process, encourages customer to stay on platform, improves price transparency, gathers platform orders, and speeds up shipment.

(3) Supporting services for the upstream and downstream ecospheres are made available, such as home appliance installation and warranty, so as to better assure the buyers.

### *"Fine business, products, and services"*

The infrastructure provided by the platform enables enterprises to think and explore their own core competitiveness in a more relaxing way without investing all resources in the supply chain. The limited resources of enterprises can be used more intensively. And more attention can be paid to team marketing, the improvement of staff skills, how to grasp the needs of overseas buyers, and how to build the core value and competitiveness of enterprises. This would accelerate enterprise transformation and innovation, so as to make it possible to gradually build individual enterprise competitiveness.

The core of individual competitiveness is "fine business, products, and service." In the future, Chinese enterprises in international trade should take the initiative to play the leading role of branding, cultivating new export competitive advantages with technology, branding, quality and service as the core, creating "fine business, products, and services," promoting the sharing of Chinese brands with the world, and reflecting China service, China quality, and China responsibility.

As a "fine business," deep involvement in foreign trade is necessary as well as the capability to lead the foreign trade industry and represent the most cutting-edge power of global suppliers. It should have effective e-commerce service, strong R & D and design, productive production and manufacturing, and deep service awareness.

As a "fine product," the product itself should show a responsible attitude towards global buyers. It should be buyer-friendly, eco-friendly and quality-friendly as well as reflect the design capacity, production capacity and technological strength of Chinese enterprises.

As "fine service," Chinese suppliers shall provide definite service based on the buyer's demand. China's fine business model, technological achievements, innovation power, and civilization concept will be spread out with the Chinese enterprises, Chinese goods and Chinese brands go overseas. The concept of China's achievement for global shared development is in practice.

Chinese suppliers heed more to improving the technological content and added value of products. As of March 2018, Alibaba.com had collected 48,000 new certificates from suppliers, including 24,000 product certificates, 16,000 patent certificates, and 9,600 trademark certificates. Although there are still problems and gaps between Chinese foreign trade enterprises and local brands, there is great promise for China with strong domestic brands. The efforts of enterprise will eventually lead to the transformation from Made-in-China to China-made.

---

**CASE STUDIES**   "Big industry:" building a pool of fine businesses

"Big industry" is one of the four industries that the Alibaba international station industry operation focuses on. The international station integrates the products and business resources of the whole industrial supply chain and establishes a large industrial professional platform of an aggregation of buyers and sellers.

- Buyer's mind: the industrial product buyers have a clear purpose of purchasing. They value professionalism of the product supplier, efficiently inquire for the product to improve the willingness of searching, pay attention to the professionalism of the businessmen in the industry, expect to establish a long-term cooperative relationship with the businessmen, and have high requirements for the product quality.
- Business insight: most of the industrial products enterprises and websites in the market are self-employed. They control the quality and goods to realize the certainty of the buyer's demand. The types of industrial products buyers are relatively complex, including factories, distributors, enterprises, etc., whose needs should be satisfied with different forms of products. For this reason, Alibaba implements the leading strategy of "professional infrastructure + professional operation."

(1) Create an SPU commodity pool to improve the efficiency of large industry search and matching with the commodity standards of SPU; strengthen the search process, guide the purchase path with graphical categories, and highlight professionalism.

(2) In the online exhibition, the buyer and seller's serious access system is implemented to improve the matching efficiency with the buyer's identity verification and selected KA sellers in the industry, as well as the matching services such as inspection and logistics, so as to promote the online order of serious buyers and sellers.

(3) Mine the top businesses in the industry, set a benchmark; cultivate KA businesses in the industry, improve the service of sellers and the conversion rate of online orders and deposit transaction data.

\*   \*   \*

## The protagonist of the times

This is a new time full of opportunities for SMEs in China.

### *China-made*

Chinese goods have a long history of going abroad. During the Western Han Dynasty, Zhang Qian, as an envoy, travelled westwards opening up the land Silk Road; at the same time, a maritime Silk Road starting from ports such as Xuwen port and Hepu port in China became a world trade network. At the beginning of the 21st century, with China's accession to the WTO, made-in-China commodities spread all over the world. The country has become an important engine for the rapid development of the world economy. In recent years, driven by China's industrial transformation and upgrading, as well as supply reform, China's commodity exports have to evolve from made-in-China to created-in-China and intelligently-manufactured-in-China. Branding has stepped closer to the center of attention. Only when we establish our own brand can we have more say.

On December 22, 2017, there are 28 countries' brands in the "2017 Top 500 World Brands" list released by the world brand laboratory. In terms of the national distribution of the number of brands, the United States accounts for 233; those of France and the United Kingdom occupy 40 and 39 seats, ranking second and third respectively. Japan, China, Germany, Switzerland and Italy huddle in the second layer, with 38, 37, 26, 21, and 14 brands selected. Although 37 Chinese brands made the cuts, Chinese brands still lag behind, contrary to the status as the world's second largest population of 1.3 billion and GDP.

Made-in-China products are all over the world, but Chinese brands didn't rise to fame as well. This contradiction has attracted great attention of the Party and the government. It was pointed out that there is great urgency to push made-in-China to transform into created-in-China, China speeds into China quality, and China products to China brand in May 2014 when President Xi Jinping visited Henan. On October 12, 2017, China-made was officially launched. The Foreign Trade Development Affairs Bureau of the Ministry of Commerce of the People's Republic of China will build a platform according to the "China-made" brand work plan. With the help of 57 trade promotion work networks around the world, it intends to show the world China products, China quality, China standards and China innovation, interpret the "hard power" and "soft power" of Chinese brands, and promote China's transformation from a trading giant to a trading power.

"China-made" is the integration, refinement, and sublimation of the concepts of "made in China," "intelligently manufactured in China," and "quality manufactured in China." How to properly apply a brand marketing strategy to participate in the competition in the new environment is a new topic for every foreign trade enterprise and entrepreneur.

## *The rise of a nobody*

In 2015, the export volume of the private economy exceeded that of foreign-funded enterprises for the first time, accounting for 45.2%, thus becoming the main body of foreign trade. Most of the foreign-funded export enterprises take processing as the principal business, which is at the low end of the global value chain. The management mechanism of the private enterprises is flexible. In addition, they have a strong adaptability to the environment. And rise of the private foreign trade enterprises as nobodies will improve the level of China's foreign trade in terms of innovation awareness, profitability, and business competence.

Simultaneously with the rise of cross-border e-commerce, micro, small- and medium-sized enterprises and consumers are becoming the new main body and driving force of globalization. With the help of the Internet and information technology, the times has been enabling nobody-enterprises. Micro, small- and medium-sized enterprises stand on the same starting line as large ones, exhibiting their unique advantages:

(1) Break the monopoly of large companies and have a fair start. The digital transaction mode of the cross-border B2B e-commerce platform reduces the transaction costs and lowers the bar of cross-border transaction participants. A large number of micro, small- and medium-sized enterprises based on cross-border collaboration of digital platforms launch products to the global market on virtual networks and virtual shelves on the platform. Hundreds of millions of buyers directly complete cross-border consumption on the platform, and a large number of small- and medium-sized manufacturers have become direct sellers in the transactions.

The cross-border e-commerce platform breaks the channel monopoly of traditional large enterprises and transnational companies. And SMEs are allowed to act as an active participant in international trade and enter the global value chain.

(2) A flat organizational structure makes it easier for rapid iterative innovation. Micro, small- and medium-sized enterprises face buyers or retailers directly on the Internet platform to master the first-hand information of demand-end changes. With a flat organizational structure, they can quickly respond to the feedback of consumption received and carry out iterative innovation on products in time, therefore constantly meeting the new needs of buyers and lifting their position in the international trade market.

(3) A deep understanding of the long-tail market together with flexible and precise strategy. In the direct interaction and transaction between suppliers from different countries and regions and accurate positioning, manufacturers will gain unique positions and competitive advantages in the market via the platform. The fragmentation of cross-border transaction buyers and sellers as well as the massive number of transactions make a valuable asset. Micro, small- and medium-sized enterprises can deeply explore the long-tail market of specific groups, produce more "small yet beautiful" products, and formulate more accurate market strategies. The insights generated by massive consumption data analysis will benefit the sellers, service providers on the platform, and even the government departments with more refined product design, marketing, and transactions and higher return on input and output.

(4) Light asset mode with low-cost global operation. The online digital platform enables enterprises to break the traditional step-by-step process of product output to cross-border sales to cross-border production and operation and to global operation. And online channel transactions, offline delivery of logistics

and after-sales service make it possible to quickly globalize business processes in the fashion of light assets. In addition, a large number of transactions and services are concentrated on the electronic platform, so that crowdfunding services can be provided at a very low cost. The development of cross-border e-commerce can push more micro, small- and medium-sized enterprises to participate in the globalization extensively via digitalization and push globalization to develop towards a more equal and inclusive direction, so that more people can enjoy the dividends that come with globalization.

In the past, for the industry "6 + 1" industrial chain (product design, raw material procurement, warehouse and transportation, order processing, wholesale operation, terminal retail plus manufacturing), China only controlled "2 + 1", i.e. raw material procurement, warehouse and transportation plus manufacturing. Instead, the United States and other developed countries controlled both ends of the "smile curve" of product design, order processing, wholesale operation, terminal retail, etc. In the future, the times will open more opportunities to a great many SMEs. They will participate in global trade with the help of the e-commerce platform, face customers directly, climb from the lower end of the global value chain to the higher end, and finally realize the global network layout. By building their own global value chain, they will develop from labor-intensive to technology-intensive; manufacturing enterprises participating in international trade with the help of platforms bypass the middlemen, reduce costs, and improve profit margin by optimizing the supply chain.

Iterative innovation supported by the platform allows China's nobody enterprises to participate in the whole global supply chain with a louder voice.

## *Brands going abroad*

In the eyes of the world, the negativity of anti-globalization and the "trade war" lingers. Today's world is experiencing a new round of great development, great change, and great adjustment. The economic globalization of the past two or three decades has brought prosperity to the world economy as well as new problems and difficulties. But it is these problems and difficulties that have opened a window of great opportunities to emerging markets, enterprises, and young people.

China has put forward the Belt and Road Initiative. It has speeded up the entry into WTO's The Government Procurement Agreement. It has convened the first China International Import fair. The actions are the determination of China's reform and opening up, the confidence of surviving in the sea of commerce, and the opportunity for Chinese enterprises to participate in the next round of globalization.

As a manufacturing giant, China has a strong manufacturing capacity. The number of manufacturing enterprises has reached the tens of millions. These enterprises are potential foreign trade enterprises. They heed more to product innovation and quality improvement. As a result, thoughts on how to move to a broader overseas market have blossomed.

New times comes with a new mission. This is the best time for foreign trade enterprises.

"In today's world, the trend of peaceful cooperation marches forward. Peace and development are the common aspiration of people all over the world. Cold war thinking and zero-benefit game are becoming growingly outdated. Arrogance or isolation can only lead to failure. Only by adhering to peaceful development and working together can we truly achieve win-win results and multiple-win results."[1]

The win-win cooperation ecology created by new foreign trade is a foreign trade pattern that utilizes the technical characteristics of the Internet, complies with the principles of openness, equality, and fairness, enables the largest range of factor participation, and constantly stimulates the creativity and innovation of different minds by building an ecosphere. SMEs should hold the mission-driven faith, actively participate in the wave of opening up, strengthen the cooperation of ecosphere, and promote the development of consumption globalization.

"In today's world, the trend of openness and blending marches forward. The history of the development of human society teaches us that opening brings progress while closing is bound to lag behind. The world has become a global village with you in me and me in you. Economic and social development of all countries are increasingly linked and influenced by each other. Promoting connectivity and accelerating integrated development have become an inevitable choice for promoting common prosperity and development."[2]

---

1. Cited from the speech *Open up to co-create prosperity and innovate to lead the future* that President Xi Jinping gave at the opening ceremony of the 2018 annual meeting of the Boao forum for Asia in Boao, Hainan.

2. Cited from the speech *Open up to co-create prosperity and innovate to lead the future* given by President Xi Jinping at the opening ceremony of the 2018 annual meeting of the Boao forum for Asia in Boao, Hainan.

New foreign trade makes use of cross-border e-commerce platforms to expand supplier resources. "Global buying and selling" came true because of vertical operation, content-based shopping guides, and intensive services of the industry. The transformation of new foreign trade mode is complete by using emerging technologies and big data. It promotes interconnection, accelerates integration development, and better pushes forward the prosperity and development of global trade. SMEs take advantage of the new foreign trade opportunities to deliver good products and technologies to global buyers through convenient and efficient Internet platform channels. Consequently, the new transformation and development of Chinese foreign trade enterprises are realized.

"In today's world, the trend of change and innovation marches forward. As early as 2,500 years ago, the ancestors of China came to an understanding that what is new can totally replace what is old as it is beneficial as needed. Reform and innovation are the fundamental driving forces for the development of human society. Whoever rejects change and innovation will lag behind the times and be eliminated by history."[1]

New foreign trade uses data to bring new technology, new thinking, and new approaches. These greatly improve the operation efficiency of foreign trade, reduces the transformation cost of foreign trade enterprises, and constantly improves the level of China's foreign trade and endows Chinese enterprises with positive energy. SMEs should also comply with the trends of the times, take advantage of the development momentum of cross-border B2B e-commerce platforms, innovate independently, deepen services, pay attention to the construction of wireless terminals, multimedia content, and specialization, and realize the qualitative leap in trade quality and trade efficiency.

The dream takes it as far as one dares.

This is the time of inclusive sharing. Internet and data support Chinese foreign trade enterprises to build new advantages.

This is the time of the rise of nobodies. Small- and medium-sized foreign trade enterprises will win back the voice and realize brand value.

And every foreign trader will be the protagonist of this time.

---

1. Cited from the speech *Open up to co-create prosperity and innovate to lead the future* by President Xi Jinping, at the opening ceremony of the 2018 annual meeting of the Boao forum for Asia in Boao, Hainan.

# PART II

# CHINESE SUPPLIERS

# CHAPTER IV

# Transformation of Traditional Foreign Trade

"INFORMATIZATION HAS BENEFITED THE Chinese nation with a once-in-a-lifetime opportunity," said General Secretary Xi Jinping when addressing the impact of Internet development on China at the National Conference on Network Security and Informatization in April 21, 2018. For a long time, China has been a cheap and low-end world factory in the international trade division system. After the rise of the e-commerce platform, Chinese sellers and global buyers are more closely connected than ever before. In this great revolution, traditional SMEs seize the opportunity to connect online and offline production while the enterprises themselves have completed an all-round upgrading and transformation, such as the improvement of production patterns, the reconstruction of brands, the enhancement of internal management, etc. That is the new vitality.

A growing number of budding small- and medium-sized foreign trade enterprises have given rise to self-consciousness of their owners as they trade with overseas customers. They actively fulfill more corporate responsibilities and establish a more proactive and positive image of Chinese suppliers overseas.

These changes from inside to outside indicate that traditional SMEs have undergone a profound transformation in the era of Internet foreign trade.

\* \* \*

## Flexible manufacturing

In the mining machinery industry, workshops in factories are commonly full of equipment, waiting for customers to pick up at any time. Qingzhou Keda Mining Machinery Co., Ltd. (Qingzhou Keda) is one exception, as its workshops are full or empty at times and orders large or small at times. The production seems unambitious except the results say otherwise. In less than three years at foreign trade, the export volume increased from RMB five million in 2015 to exceed RMB 13 million in 2016, and then to RMB 30 million in 2017. The company has a good momentum of development and ranks in the top five in the country in respect of overall strength.

How does a traditional factory, which is used to domestic trade and has no overseas customer resources, make a rapid breakthrough after making use of the Internet platform to transform itself for foreign trade? According to Lun Guan'an, head of the International Trade Department of Qingzhou Keda, the secret lies in the change of the production mode of mass production and homogeneous delivery that many manufacturers in the traditional foreign trade export prefer, by using Internet big data to guide the factory to carry out flexible manufacturing. The downstream market demand is therefore more closely linked with the upstream production, which forces the transformation and upgrading of the old factory, so as to expand production capacity rapidly.

During China's National People's Congress (NPC) and the Chinese People's Political Consultative Conference (CPPCC) in 2015, Feng Fei, director of Industrial Policy Division of China's Ministry of Industry and Information Technology, expressed the idea that the combination of the Internet and manufacturing technology is an important tool to overcome the current difficulties in manufacturing industry and realizing the dream of "Made-in-China 2025" as a manufacturing power when proposing the Internet + plan for the first time in the Government Work Report.

### Premise of flexible manufacturing and understanding of customer needs

The so-called flexible manufacturing refers to a supply chain with enough flexibility and a production capacity able to react quickly according to the market demand.

"But only if we really understand the needs of our customers," stressed Lun.

Qingzhou Keda started as a factory of iron separation equipment. And it has always been only engaged in domestic trade. As the domestic market approached saturation in 2011, it sought transformation. Fortunately, the factory later developed gold panning equipment, holding patents from product design to appearance. And the market responded well to the launch of the product. At that time, there happened to be another gold rush wave in Africa. In 2015, the factory began to engage in foreign trade on the Internet platform and explore new markets.

However, it had no experience back then. After a year's hard work, the sales volume of foreign trade reached only RMB five million. What left a deep impression on Lun is that at that time, domestic products were directly exported without considering the needs of overseas customers. Once the salesman sent a picture of the finished equipment to an Ecuadorian customer thinking that the other party would be very satisfied. However, the customer gave over ten opinions at one go, including poor paint spraying, poor welding appearance quality, rough grinding, etc. "It was not until that talked with the customer did we realize that foreign customers paid attention to both practicality and appearance. And they would like to have their money well spent by receiving products that meet all of their requirements."

Later, the factory completely improved the appearance and processing as required and eventually satisfied the Ecuadorian customers. This deal greatly inspired Qingzhou Keda. Then, the big data provided by Alibaba's back-end operation and their own customer service tracking lead to the finding that in the export of mining machinery, overseas customers who value both quality and appearance like this one are not individual cases, but common. This is a completely different client mentality from the Chinese market. So Qingzhou Keda of began to set up a professional foreign trade team to render targeted foreign trade sales services.

Different from the strategy of the whole domestic ore industry's careless understanding customers' needs, Qingzhou Keda has also learned about the needs based on customer feedback and big data analysis. It independently created a set of detailed and comprehensive customer background survey forms in the industry. Before each customer made a purchase of the equipment, the salesman would ask the other party to do a questionnaire survey. The question settings are differentiated according to the different equipment. The content of the questionnaire has been gradually enlarged from the first ten items to the next 20 or 30. The most suitable products can only be recommended according to the budget of the other parties after their needs are clearly understood.

Lun acknowledged that foreign trade may become more complicated this way, but it could accurately figure out the needs of customers and leave a very professional impression on them. Otherwise, a piece of equipment that can easily cost tens of thousands or hundreds of thousands of dollars may turn out useless for a customer, who would naturally draw the conclusion that Chinese products are poor. "So we must do our job well first."

### Flexible manufacturing, from mass production to order production

Flexible manufacturing is also different from mass production. The traditional way of foreign trade is to produce a batch of equipment to be sold no matter whether the market needs it or not.

Lun disclosed that the advantage of hoarding inventory is that in case of urgent need of customers, goods can be immediately shipped, but there will be no advantage in price. After all, the factory needs to convert every piece of equipment into current capital as soon as possible, otherwise the equipment will be under the

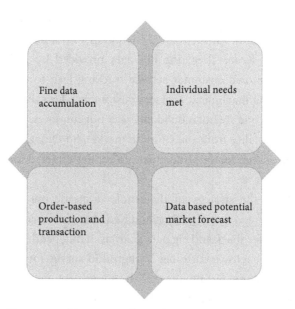

**Figure 4.1** Characteristics of flexible manufacturing

pressure of inventory cost. At this time, overseas customers will naturally take the opportunity to bargain, "because you are not the only one with the supply."

Flexible manufacturing refers to order production, which meets the market's demand fully according to the customers. In the workshops of Qingzhou Keda, when there are more orders, the equipment fills the space, and when there none, they are empty. Even if there is some early production, it's not a blind decision but after a market analysis based on big data and comprehensive customer feedback, so as to make an early layout of the market with potential needs. For example, when a new customer is developed in South Africa, the factory will produce two or three pieces of semi-finished equipment in a semi-customized manner according to the characteristics of the South African market once receiving positive feedback from the customer. When a similar order is placed again in South Africa, rapid production and delivery can be achieved.

In 2017, Qingzhou Keda also had a cross-border experience, exporting environmental protection equipment such as mower boats to African and Southeast Asian markets as the principal products, which is also a targeted production based on big data analysis. Practices have proved the production mode according to the buyer's demand of this factory to be very successful as the new sales volume of environmental protection equipment accounts for about 30% of the whole factory's annual sales volume.

**Figure 4.2** Harvesters exported to South Africa

Although it was long time since the company entered into foreign trade, Lun felt the change of the industry. Once upon a time, a single order could amount to several million RMB, but since the first half of 2017, the order of small single was close to 60%. And an order of several hundred thousand RMB is considered one with a large amount. He believes that following the trend of order miniaturization, flexible production is to make personalized products.

Before, Qingzhou Keda, like most factories in the mining machinery industry, had only one or two types of products for one type of equipment. However, after flexible production, it is different. Each type of equipment has many personalized products according to different needs and geographical conditions. Taking the newly developed environmental protection equipment mower boat as an example, it can be further divided into water hyacinth mower, algae mower, weeds mower, garbage collection mower, etc. The categories of equipment will be expanded. Specific to each type of product, there are different function choices according to the needs of users in different countries. For example, some customers require the mower to mow the watergrass, some require mowing and recovering the watergrass together, and some require more, hoping to recover and classify the garbage at the same time. A variety of production is customized fully according to customer needs.

## Flexible manufacturing forces old factories to upgrade and transform

As the trend of foreign trade order personalization prevails, overseas buyers are no longer satisfied with customization only based on different specifications of components, but also require full customization from appearance to function. The fact that buyers become more particular forces upstream factories to perform flexible manufacturing in components, raw materials, and other aspects.

The effect by Internet + foreign trade on old factories can also be noticed in the development of Qingzhou Keda. The factory started from iron separation, sand screening, and rinsing equipment, and later developed two kinds of patented products: gold mining equipment and dredgers. In 2017, the market demand guided the increasing production of environmental protection equipment. Witnessing the continuous adaptation of the factory to the changes in customer demand, Lun concluded that the continuous upgrading and transformation of the market and foreign trade environment made it happen. If the factory had stayed

**Figure 4.3** Gold digger and dredger of Keda

at the initial stage of the export of iron separation equipment, it could not have developed so fast.

Production technology applied in the factory has increased significantly, an obvious change as Lun sees it. Since individualized production has become mainstream, it can no longer produce a batch of equipment according to the same mechanical drawing as before. Instead, a drawing is required for every single piece of equipment. In addition, drawing design involves different attention to customers' different needs in fine appearance or quality. As time passes by, the technological content of the factory will naturally increase. Even its star product gold panning equipment is no longer fixed after receiving the invention patent, but constantly improve the appearance and practicability of the product on the basis of customer's feedback. The gold panning equipment exported to Canada had its granularity and efficiency of gold extraction significantly improved to extract 20 grams of gold on a daily basis after improving the workmanship as requested by customers. This experience also greatly impressed Qingzhou Keda. "If every old factory insists on upgrading and transformation in line with the constant changes and demands of the terminal market in upstream production, foreign trade will no longer be difficult and the products will certainly not be eliminated."

To sum up, flexible manufacturing refers to a supply chain with enough flexibility and a production capacity to be able to respond quickly to the market demand. Orders of mass production are feasible, so are orders of personalized production, and the quality of both kinds of orders can be unified and controllable. In addition to the production end, flexible manufacturing can also force upstream factories to carry out flexible production, thus promoting their upgrading and transformation.

For enterprises, the biggest advantage of flexible manufacturing is to seize the sales opportunity without causing inventory risk while greatly increasing the space for profit. In this respect, Lun has a deep understanding. He recalled that before 2011, the benefit of the whole mining machinery industry in China was relatively satisfying and the profit of mass production was relatively high. In the era of foreign trade by Internet, mass production is no longer the mainstream of foreign trade export and the profit of mining machinery industry has declined significantly, hovering from 10% to 15% at most. However, Qingzhou Keda experienced a rapid growth in profits to at least 25% thanks to the production required by the orders. It is believed that as Internet penetrates into foreign trade more deeply in the future, the profit gap between flexible production based on big data and traditional mass production will extend wider.

*   *   *

## Building a brand

Every employee at the Qingdao Haiyi Hair Products Co., Ltd. is aware of a batch of defective hair wefts worth more than RMB 400,000 stocked in the warehouse, some of which have been cut apart by the boss.

It was the second year since Cao Qiyun engaged in foreign trade. A bath of hair wefts shipped to Europe were damaged due to improper dyeing operations of workers. But at that time, the workers who were used to the process, product managers, and some family members believed that this was merely a technical error within a reasonable range and that the goods could be delivered as usual. Cao was so angry that he started a dispute with the workers. When the two sides were in a standoff at the workshop, he made a decision. He picked up the scissors on the spot and cut the hair wefts: "I will cover for the loss myself without charging you guys one penny."

Many years later, Cao's company has four production lines and over 1000 professional production workers, ranking among the top ten wigs companies in Qingdao. Recalling the story at the workshop, he never regretted it. "My products are not allowed to have any defects. When the customer chooses me, I choose to be responsible to deserve the trust."

Two generations of Cao's family are engaged in foreign trade of wigs while his father's generation only dealt with the processing of wigs, a typical labor-intensive production. With great importance attached to quality, he built a brand and is making it bigger through the Internet. Now in Qingdao, there are a large number of young people like Cao. They have gathered on the Alibaba platform and generated an overall brand effect on Qingdao wig industry.

In 2018, China welcomed the 40th anniversary of reform and opening up. In the past four decades, Cao, a representative of Qingdao wig industry's growth, is the epitome of Chinese small- and medium-sized foreign trade enterprises growing from nobody to somebody.

### *Regional aggregation of industries and industrial brand effect*

China is certainly a wig factory in the world, producing more than 80% of the world's wig products. There are three wig production bases: Xuchang, Henan Province; Qingdao, Shandong Province; and Taihe, Anhui Province. But their development models are different. Until now, it is still traditional processing and production with only a few engaged in foreign trade in Taihe. Xuchang is mainly engaged in mass production, with the majority of entrepreneurs in their 50s and 60s, who are not very thrilled about the use of e-commerce platforms. In contrast, wig production in Qingdao is the most dynamic. Most of the owners were born in the 1980s and 1990s. They are young and feel emboldened to try new things. As early as 2006, some of them began to use e-commerce platforms.

Born in 1986, Cao is one of the young bosses. He grew up in a traditional wig business family. In the early years, his father walked around the streets searching for a barber shop, where he bought the hair that was neatly cut and took it home for processing, and then sold it to a state-owned wig export company in Qingdao to earn some profits. Later, the state-owned company closed down. Some former employees flew solo exporting wigs. Cao's father became their supplier. It can be said that no matter who the buyer is, he stayed in the processing and production business.

In the aftermath of global financial crisis in 2008, major foreign customers reduced their orders. The wig industry in Qingdao was deeply affected. And his father's business took a big blow. The next year, Cao, who was studying abroad, returned home to help him manage the small factory. At that time, he and many young people in Qingdao realized that it was necessary to use the Internet to open a new sales channel. In 2011, Cao became a member of the Alibaba platform and began to participate in the most important transformation and upgrading of the local wig industry.

"In fact, all kinds of wigs businesses were happening in Qingdao at the beginning." A person in charge of Alibaba's operation in Qingdao recalled that it was a large number of young e-businessmen in Qingdao active on the Internet at that time who led them to decide to take the advantages of the Internet to help them develop markets and locate brand positioning.

### *Specialized production service as the foundation of brand*

When Cao decided to fly solo, one of the big reasons was that he had different production concepts from his father. "My father wants to produce. A timely delivery of goods is his pursuit. He doesn't care if there are any defects." Cao doesn't agree with his point of view. He believes that only by making the best products can we establish the core advantages of a brand.

It was very difficult to conduct foreign trade on the Internet at the beginning. He and his wife received no inquiries nor understood the operation of e-commerce platform. They only posted advertisements every day before going offline at 2 or 3 A.M. It was not until half a year later that they met a Ukrainian customer, who is a big fish in the local area except that he had just entered the wig industry thus unfamiliar with the situation. Eventually, he initially selected 10 Chinese sellers for investigation according to their responsiveness and communication regarding his inquiries.

He also met with Cao when he investigated the goods on the spot in Qingdao. Although Cao's car was shabby when he picked up the customer at the airport, unlike other manufacturers who were younger and drove fancier cars, the Ukrainian found that he was very familiar with the industry when he showed him the goods. Cao knew every production link like the back of his band. And he also had his own set of thinking and design concepts on how to complete the production with high quality as the buyer requires. The customers finally made the deal with Cao, one worth RMB one million.

After Cao and his wife earned the big order, they made headlines in Qingdao foreign trade circle. Many believed they were lucky, hitting a jackpot. Behind the victory, only Cao knew that the real reason for landing the Ukrainian customers was he saw a totally different professionalism from the owners who only do process products on behalf of others.

Specialized production enables Cao to stand out in the whole industry. The concept has laid a solid foundation for Cao to develop his own brand from now on.

### *Adherence to the principle of quality makes great performance*

The first pot of gold built Cao's confidence. He decided to expand the production scale, increasing the number of workers to 2300. Soon, he was confronted with a new challenge: how to ensure that the quality of products in the production meets his expectations.

At that time, most of the hirable workers in Qingdao were former employees working in processing factories. Although they are skilled, they tended to treat Cao's orders with the standards applied in the factories before, thus often are unhappy with Cao's higher-standard requirements. Take the hair wefts incident as an example. After the products were finished, they believed that those defects were normal enough for a processing factory, especially since the former boss never complained but delivered them as usual. Cao's family also saw as not a big problem after checking them. They advised him with immediate shipment.

But Cao felt uneasy. Looking at these products, he was in a dilemma. Shipping them would leave the customer unsatisfied, therefore possibly no more orders from him; Keeping them, who will make up for the loss? After all, RMB 400,000 is a lot of money. He recalled the situation, "I am actually a serious person, and I will never tolerate defective products under my nose delivered to customers. But the workers and production managers failed to realize it at all."

Failing to have the idea accepted, Cao suddenly took a pair of scissors from the workshop in front of all the worker and cut some of the defective hair wefts into pieces. Immediately, he announced that the order was forbidden to be delivered and all would be redone. The decision astonished everyone, especially the workers who realized for the first time that he was not the same as the former owners of the processing factory. Cao then fully took over production and personally inspected the quality. The strict boss also added a new provision in the labor contract that when workers fail to make products due to their own mistakes, they may at worst be sued for Cao's loss of reputation. The attitude of workers towards production has completely changed since then and the rate of unqualified products has also decreased significantly.

In the second half of 2012, Cao, a perfectionist, once again improved the production process of a hair weft product mainly oriented at the UK market. Unexpectedly, when the goods arrived in the UK, they immediately sold out. In that year, the export volume of the factory soared to RMB 20 million. After the company entered the track of rapid development, he struck while the iron was hot, launching two popular products, to a very positive market response. In 2013, the export volume doubled to RMB 40 million, and in 2014, it doubled again to RMB 80 million.

### Persistence in quality in a chaotic industry

As the export of Qingdao wig enterprises like Cao's on e-commerce platform increasingly thrived, in 2014 a group of young entrepreneurs began to join. The number of Qingdao wig foreign trade factories on the Alibaba platform has surged from a dozen in the past to several thousand. Some companies have only one employee yet are bold enough to sell wigs. The quality of companies in the industry is naturally uneven. Take Shunfa products as an example. Cao, who persists in good quality, keeps using 100% real hair. However, many deliberately mixed fake hair to reduce costs, which made it difficult for foreign customers to identify the authenticity of the product.

Teeth are exposed when the lips are lost. As the foreign trade order of e-commerce platform became worse, Cao was inevitably affected. In 2015, the company stopping making rapid progress, and its export volume was only over 100 million yuan, with a growth rate significantly lower than before. In 2016, the growth rate was not very significant.

At this time, the Alibaba platform began a new round of upgrading and transformation, from a simple information display platform to a trading platform

**Table 4.1** Annual export growth of Haiyi (By RMB)

| Year | Export volume |
| --- | --- |
| 2012 | 20 million |
| 2013 | 40 million |
| 2014 | 80 million |
| 2015 | 100 million |
| ...... | |
| 2017 | 300 million |

and launched a credit guarantee system. The credit guarantee system mainly endorses those regular enterprises with good credit and excellent product quality. At that time, Qingdao Jiaozhou wig industry, which was in a mess in the industry, was lucky to become the first pilot area of credit-assured trade in China. In the process, a large number of small companies with no strength and poor products soon collapsed.

Cao seized the opportunity to pay more attention to product quality while encouraging salesmen and overseas buyers to adopt the credit assurance trading system. Soon, his average number of credit-assured orders was 1430% higher than the industry average, and the delivery volume of OneTouch was 5000% higher than the industry average. The big data analysis and transformation of the Alibaba platform helped him to obtain more overseas big customers with real purchasing demand and to locate suitable buyers.

After completing the survival of the fittest in the credit assurance system and re-aggregating the industry resources with strength and brand effect, Alibaba began to promote Qingdao wigs in a targeted manner around the world. In addition to the intention to increase publicity on the website, Alibaba also reached an agreement with the express companies. Not only is the delivery fee per transaction at least RMB 60 cheaper than that of Xuchang, a great logistics cost reduction, but next-day arrival service for international goods was launched as wigs are fast-moving consumer goods (FMCGs) with the characteristics of timeliness. In this way, Chinese sellers can ship goods on Monday morning and American buyers can receive them on Tuesday, a great improvement for the turnover rate of goods.

Taking advantage of these favorable conditions, the wig industry in Qingdao soon regained prosperity.

### Customized innovation builds brand core competitiveness

This industry has experienced a full makeover, which really opened a new chapter of development for wig industry in Qingdao, Shandong Province. Big data analysis on the Internet helped Qingdao bosses to realize that overseas buyers show obviously more interest in hand-hooked wigs, so they began to concentrate on making those. This kind of product, totally different from pure processing as substitute labor, requires design and technological content, thus more significant profit is. After optimizing the production, Qingdao wigs firmly occupied the high-end market in Europe, America, and Africa. Cao also enjoyed the benefits of the

**Figure 4.4** Haiyi exhibition stand in Atlanta, USA

overall optimization of the market environment. With a focus on European and American markets, his company's export volume reached nearly RMB 300 million in 2017.

The wig industry is special. Everyone with different facial shapes and skin colors demand different wigs. It's impossible to meet all their requirement with one type of product. After 2016, the Internet has penetrated deeper into the industry, making prices transparent and competitions fiercer. At this time, individual efforts to improve the quality of products can no longer create immediately-sold-out products. Especially in the past two years, there has been a new trend in foreign trade: private customization. The personalized orders of overseas buyers have increased significantly. As an industry of FMCGs, the changes in this aspect are more obvious. Among Cao's orders, the small customized products account for about 40%, and the number of hair shade colors has also grown from ten when he first started the business to over 60 now. Behind the changes, higher requirements were naturally put forward for the production in the factory. For example, many

**Figure 4.5** New product development discussion by the Haiyi technology R & D team

processes needed to be added to make the color change naturally and gradually to meet the high-quality needs of overseas buyers.

Now, Cao has to rely on big data analysis to accurately predict the market. Haiyi has special market analysts, data analysts, an R & D department and a design department. "I think it would never happen in the future that a product becomes popular only because of me." In March 2018, the company was very united, with 196 new customers and a turnover of US$1.74 million, ranking first in the same industry in China during the new trade festival held on Alibaba platform.

In the past, China attracted a large number of labor-intensive industries by virtue of its large population and low production costs, but at that time, made-in-China meant cheap and low-end internationally. In the past seven years, Cao has actively abandoned the processing production mode represented by his father as a substitute labor and embraced the e-commerce platform for foreign trade. He insisted on quality production, built his own brand, used big data analysis on the Internet to capture the new trends of overseas buyers, and eventually completed the optimization in the entire industrial chain.

It can be said that Qingdao wigs make full use of Internet resources and provide a new reference path for the transformation and development of traditional labor-intensive industries in China.

* * *

# Chinese positive energy

In the 2017 hit drama *In the Name of People*, Cai Chenggong, the factory director of Dafeng factory, is slick and sly. He bids by any means. For quite a long time, it was common that people like him, to maximize profits, engaged in price competition and vicious scheming. However, with a growing number of SMEs, they begin to consciously assume social responsibility and play the role of new suppliers transmitting Chinese positive energy in foreign trade.

The ancient Chinese philosopher Lao Tzu once said that to take, one must give. These have been words to live by for Tang Libin, general manager of Dehui (Dalian) International Trade Co., Ltd., who witnessed the leap of China's foreign trade from 1.0 to 3.0. By 2017, the export volume of his company had reached US$22 million, with customers in 55 countries and regions around the world. In the process, Tang has been very proud that as a Chinese supplier, he can constantly convey the patriotism of an entrepreneur overseas.

## *The realization of the significance of work*

Tang's foreign trade started as early as 1992. In the primary stage, he was engaged in the export of APIs (Active Pharmaceutical Ingredients), and some of the anti-malaria APIs were shipped to Africa. When it comes to malaria, Chinese are now unfamiliar. The disease has been completely eradicated in the country. However, in some third-world countries in Africa, it still threatens the lives of locals. Take Nigeria, which has a high rate of malaria infection in the world, for example. In 2015 alone, more than 190,000 people died of the disease.

There is a big pharmaceutical factory in Nigeria. As soon as Tang started foreign trade, he cooperated with the pharmaceutical factory. When the drug demand was at the peak, Tang's annual export volume to the African country was nearly US$1 million. The APIs were repacked and produced there and then sold to Kenya, Ethiopia, Tanzania, and other neighboring East African countries with a high incidence of malaria.

For a long time, Tang, like every foreign trader at that time, frequently traveled back and forth to various exhibitions at home and abroad every year. Foreign trade was a profitable business for him. One day, he accidentally read in the newspaper that a well-known entrepreneur in China was suddenly infected with malaria while traveling in the remote grasslands of East Africa. At that time, the entrepreneur was badly ill. Fortunately, he found an anti-malaria drug in time and escaped death. At that time, Tang wondered whether the life-saving medicine this famous Chinese entrepreneur took was one of his exports there. The thought washed him over with a sense of meaningfulness in foreign trade.

After that, Tang took the initiative to adjust the cooperation with that pharmaceutical factory in Nigeria. When the stock of APIs is tight, he tries to meet the needs of the customer by allocating goods from other domestic manufacturers. Sometimes when Nigerian pharmaceutical companies have difficulty in capital turnover, he makes an exception to allow a payment delay for two months. In the foreign trade industry, it is a big risk to agree that customers will delay the payment for such a long time, but Tang never regrets the choice. "This kind of medicine is in great demand locally, so I am willing to continue the collaboration. And I also believe in the sales ability of that pharmaceutical factory."

Later, Tang organized a speech contest in the company according to the life-saving medicine news published in the newspaper to raise the awareness among employees to realize that their work matters a lot to a large population. Since then, the corporate culture has slowly changed. In 2012, after the Fukushima nuclear leak in Japan, the company received an emergency order to produce container houses for the staff cleaning up the nuclear leak. To send ordered goods to the earthquake-stricken areas in Japan as soon as possible, a designer of the company volunteered to work overtime every night until 2 or 3 A.M. Early in the morning, the designer woke up and continued to make the drawings. Tang said that if it wasn't driven by a sense of social responsibility, the designer would not have sustained that long in such high intensity work.

During the years of contact, the Nigerian pharmaceutical factory certainly felt the positive energy of Dalian Dehui. The partnership not only lasted for nearly 20 years but gave benefit to Tang with recommendations to other African customers. The business volume in Africa accounts for 10% of the annual export volume of the company. Recently, an Indian customer made an inquiry to Tang's company and the introducer was also the pharmaceutical factory in Nigeria. In a way, the relationship between Tang and the pharmaceutical factory has gone beyond ordinary business partnership to a higher level of mutual assistance and reciprocity.

*1% water purification equipment shares, 100% feelings*

In June 2017, Tang and a Cameroon customer agreed on a long-term order to export a clean water production line to Cameroon, where there is shortage of clean water every year.

It was an order that had been negotiated for two years. In 2015, a Cameroonian customer actively contacted Tang via the Alibaba international station, but after learning about the quotation and production plan of clean water production line from the salesman, no further contact was made. The salesman assumed the order was gone and naturally forgot about it as time went by. However, in the spring of 2017, Cameroon's customers suddenly reappeared, asking the salesman to revise the previously proposed clean water production line plan. He would come to China to inspect the goods.

It was not until they met as scheduled in Dalian that Cameroonian buyers revealed the reason for the disappearance for two years. He told Tang that Cameroon is very short of water and the national drinking water supply rate was only 50%

**Figure 4.6** Group photo with Cameroonian customers

**Figure 4.7** Signing ceremony between Tang Libin and Cameroonian buyers

in 2016. Due to the lack of sufficient clean tap water, many rural residents have to go to the river to get water by themselves. The incidence of water-borne diseases remains high. In some places, hundreds of people die of cholera every year. If there is a clean water production line, water from wells and rivers can be purified so that local people can afford clean and relatively cheap water, thus reducing the spread of diseases.

He was satisfied with the product quality and plan of Tang's company after comparing prices on the Internet. However, a complete bottled water production line with purification and packaging costs about US$300,000. Moreover, an advance payment that is 30% of the total amount has to made. The customer, with limited economic strength, can only give part of the advance payment. Later, a fundraising was launched in Christian churches, where the remaining funds were raised from 1,500 people, including teachers, priests, and residents. Eventually, they were able to afford the set of equipment from Tang.

The narrative brought Tang's wife to tears. To help local residents improve their living conditions, the couple decided to buy in 1% shares on the spot to show their support. Tang believes that although the share is not a lot of money, it delivers a message to the customer that he is determined to follow up this matter and do his best to help them improve their living conditions. Tang also told his colleagues that we must make sure that the quality of this set of equipment is the best and the cost the lowest.

Tang's actions touched the Cameroonian buyers greatly. They believe that this special clean water production line extends beyond an ordinary foreign trade deal and reflects the friendship between the people from the two countries. At the subsequent signing ceremony, he asked Tang to find him a set of traditional Chinese outfits to put on, and Tang wore the French bow tie common in Cameroon. The live feed of the signing recorded by the translators later made the local TV news in Cameroon.

### Running an online business association

Tang was engaged in traditional foreign trade for 11 years until the outbreak of SARS in 2003. All domestic exhibitions were halted, many international flights cancelled, and business severely affected. By chance at this time, he noticed an Alibaba advertisement in the newspaper, so he turned to the Internet platform for foreign trade. In 2010, having been working in online foreign trade for seven years, Tang founded the Dalian E-commerce Association to help more small- and medium-sized foreign trade enterprises adapt to the characteristics of foreign trade development in the Internet era and learn internet thinking and new management approaches. The Dalian E-Commerce Association has attracted more than 120 small- and medium-sized foreign trade companies to join.

In the traditional business era, businessmen kept their business secrets. Only by keeping the secrets can they survive in the market. At the beginning of Dalian E-Commerce Association, some friends incomprehensibly asked Tang why help others when business ground is like a battlefield where helping a peer means a potential competitor. For these doubts, Tang always laughs it off without further comment. He has a longer vision. He admits despite the different categories of foreign trade industry, the management and approaches are interlinked. The problems of another company will certainly happen to his own company except they have not been found for the time being. Helping others find solutions to the problems eventually benefit his own company. In this point of view, helping others is actually helping oneself. "Besides, if the key to your company's success is easily learned and copied, it is certainly not the real key."

In 2017, Tang together with other members of the association dealt with an event of extreme employee turnover. This is also a common problem that troubles many bosses in the foreign trade industry. A boss works hard for many years, but the staff has been unstable. Often when an order has not been completed, some staff left. And the most infuriating part is that senior staff who leaves often sets up a new company and takes away a majority of customer resources. After the boss asked Tang for help, Tang and several other senior foreign traders from Dalian E-Commerce Association analyzed for him the causes of the turbulence and later gave him training courses such as team management and corporate culture nurturing. A period of training benefited the man a lot on business management. Three months later, the internal turmoil of the company began to be effectively controlled.

It is this favor that deeply enlightened Tang, that if the staff of foreign trade companies frequently change jobs, the head must first reflect on himself/herself by asking ask a couple of questions: how comfortable the working environment has been provided to employees, and whether they have given enough promotion chances and trust. If these are failed to be made available, employees naturally leave and the termination of employment would end ugly. Later, Tang made major adjustments in his company's internal management, actively delegating part of the management power, giving more space for senior staff to give full play to their talents, and increasing the contact between staff and the enterprise through the year-end dividend reform. In this way, they can enjoy more development benefits of the company.

In Tang's company, the employee with the longest employment has been there for more than 20 years. And there are five or six employees who have worked for over 10 years. They are the best witnesses of the company's growth. Over the years, his continuous active adjustment of the company's management system kept the stable employee turnover rate below 10%.

"In the era of globalization, what can Chinese small- and medium enterprises do?" This is a question that Tang often asks himself and others. He said that in the past, Chinese enterprises commonly pursued profits solely in business, among which some tried shoddy tricks and faked the products. At that time, foreign trade was profitable for the large amount of cheap labor and raw materials in the Chinese market, as well as for information asymmetry at home and abroad.

The development of the Internet has built a larger foreign trade stage for SMEs. And business order and civilization have also been gradually restored. When more made-in-China commodities are sold overseas, enterprises must take the initiative to establish a positive image and undertake more social responsibilities, so as to improve the reputation and soft power of enterprises and generate more economic benefits.

# CHAPTER V

# The Rise of the Nobodies

A FEMALE COLLEGE STUDENT born in the 90s started her own businesses shortly after graduation. Four years later, the company grew to 30 employees, with an annual export of over RMB 100 million.

A procurement director of a foreign company born in the 80s gave up the fancy job to start a business from scratch. In a mere two years, the orders increased by 305% and 380% respectively.

A college teacher born in the 70s, who had no customer resources, no sales channels, and very limited start-up capital, built an online giant through an e-commerce platform, with the export volume ranking top in the industry.

A rural woman born in the 60s who used to work as a bricklayer now owns a company as large as more than 220 square meters with an annual export of tens of millions of US dollars.

In 1999, the Alibaba platform was created to provide thousands of common entrepreneurs with a new stage and new trading opportunities. Numerous nobody-enterprises have budded and developed as an indispensable force in foreign trade that injects fresh vitality into the rapid development of China's economy.

Foreign trade is believed to be trickier than ever. Why can the nobodies rise on the Alibaba platform instead? What are the key spots in the development and change of the industry that they have stepped on to make it happen?

The development of nobody-enterprises witnesses the 19-year development of Alibaba platform. Understanding the secret behind their rise is key to understanding why Alibaba has boldly innovated by undergoing multiple major transformations.

∗   ∗   ∗

## Data empowerment

Germans are characterized by their rigor and focus on fine quality; British are very time-effective, and Scandinavians prefer a majestic style. Born in 1981, eight years of foreign trade of Computer Numerical Control (CNC) engraving enabled Sun Jinyuan to finally perceive the different needs of different customers and successfully sell products to all over the world.

From the IT era to the DT era, consumers have left massive traces on the Internet. Who are the customers? Where are they? What do they buy? Big data analysis, like GPS, helps businessmen to clearly see the market trends. The original business marketing model has therefore been completely altered. It is the opportunity of data empowerment that Sun seized to perform precise marketing and then brand management. The company has developed from a humble husband-and-wife store to a foreign trade company with 33 employees, with customers from over 100 countries and regions around the world.

### Zero resources for foreign trade = 100% reliance on network platform

Since college graduation, Sun had been engaged for several years in drug research, development, and sales. Marriage motivated him to provide for his family in a more stable manner, thus the idea of starting a business. Back then, it used to cost tens of thousands of RMB to start up a business in many industries. All his bank balances together added up to RMB 80,000, which he saved as the down payment for an apartment in Jinan.

One day in 2009, on a cab ride, the driver blabbed about some foreigners coming to Jinan to negotiate business. And all the business took place online. He thought to himself that since his wife majored in English, why not make use of it. So the woman was asked to try to export Jinan's common CNC machinery on the Internet. Sun calculated that the cost of traditional foreign trade would be too large mainly because of the high cost of information acquisition arising from the information asymmetry between the supplier and the customer. For example, if the sales of CNC mechanical engravers they produce would adopt the old-fashioned way, i.e. by exhibition, only the display of several machines on the exhibition site would cost at least RMB 150,000. Turning to online trade would save money, so they decided to rely entirely on the Internet platform for foreign trade.

In 2011, Sun also officially resigned to co-manage the company with his wife. At that time, there were only four employees in the company. They went to the factory to take photos every day and posted them together with parameters, prices, and other information on the platform both day and night. Other than that, they knew no marketing methods. The product information distribution was only following local exporters, taking Southeast Asia as the target market. As a result, there was no improvement for a couple of years. Sun didn't know the reason but assumed that the publicity was not as wide as others', therefore more investment in advertisement.

"Frankly, it was blind selling all along." Sun summed up the pattern as he recalled the difficulties in the early stage of entrepreneurship. At that time, there were countless small enterprises of similar scale on the Alibaba platform because the threshold for the entry of CNC machinery export was not high and Shandong is a major export province. Without overseas sales channels and contact resources, it was beyond difficult for him to successfully find a buyer in the vast Internet. After over two years of hard work, the business operation was still ordinary. The annual export volume was only RMB two million. With labor and other expenses deducted, there was little left.

### The help of big data: efficient matching between supply and demand

The first year of big data came in 2013. Whether it was the competition among social platforms, e-commerce, or portal websites, big data was involved. Almost all world-class Internet enterprises extended their business to the big data industry. The U.S. government's launch of a US$200 million big data R&D scheme lifted it to the national strategic level.

It was in this year that Sun first came into contact with the concept of big data analysis when he enrolled on the online business training organized by Alibaba. He realized that the advent of big data completely altered the marketing mode of foreign trade. For him, it was either to change or to be eliminated.

The traditional way of foreign trade is to find customers mainly according to the population, geographical environment, customs, and other factors. The target is vague as a whole without core competitive advantages. The new foreign trade under a big data layout is to efficiently match the demands of suppliers and customers through long-term data participation. Data analysis allows a clear view of which countries foreign trade products are exported and which markets have a great capacity. Enterprises then adopt differentiated precision marketing plans to greatly improve the order turnover rate.

Sun immediately applied a big data analysis method he learned in Alibaba to his company to re-locate the market. He picked products with similarity to his in quality, price, and positioning on the Alibaba platform and analyzed and summarized their market distribution one by one. Then, he made use of customs export data and Google search results while checking brands with similar positioning on their export countries and regions. Finally, multiple channel data analysis and comparisons led to the conclusion that the products they export are mainly middle-end and high-end. The Southeast Asian market is only in need of low-end machinery and equipment. And the real demand is actually in Europe and the United States. The fact that they marched in the wrong direction answered the question why the business had showed no improvement. "Before the big data thinking pattern, when we engaged in foreign trade, we tended to mistake the whole world for customers. It was not until later that we knew that the market should be divided very clearly." Sun summarized.

### *The help of big data: suppliers complete precision marketing*

However, the European and American market being enormous, how can Sun locate specific individual buyers?

He developed a new marketing strategy that classifies the customer groups to identify the most potential buyers, on whom precise promotion is to be made. Specifically, the approach is to analyze the keyword resources obtained in big data analysis. For example, brand words, bidding product words, related words on the industry's internal e-commerce search platform, hot words, and blue ocean words are analyzed to figure out the keywords highly related to overseas buyers' search habits. After getting these keywords, customers are categorized according to the buyer's habits of different countries and different marketing plans are adopted.

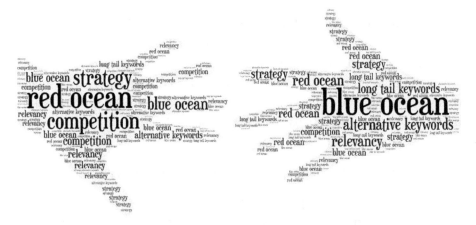

**Figure 5.1** Alibaba platform's keyword analysis

For instance, as Germans are rigorous, the products must be professional; Nordic people are fond of fancy product appearance, the mechanical appearance design of the exports must be perfected. Once everything is in place, when overseas buyers make inquiries, a salesmen can implement targeted marketing plans, so that the inquiry conversion rate will naturally increase.

"Unlike many others in the same industry, our ultimate goal is not to market the products, but to provide customers with solutions to their problems," said Sun when talking about his differentiation advantages in big data applications. The perception on customer demand is also made on the basis of accumulated information from the sales and customer communication after data analysis is complete. For example, their side drilling equipment addresses the problem of keyhole drilling at door installations; the material lift is a solution to the inconvenience of moving up and down various building boards during decoration.

With the help of big data, Sun adjusted the marketing direction and measures in time. Thus, the company began to walk out of predicament and welcome new development. The export volume increased to nearly RMB four million in 2013, RMB eight million in 2014, and nearly RMB 30 million in 2017.

Sun also has adopted a big data analysis to expand into new marketing channels. He pays close attention to the new announcements and industrial trend forecasts from all directions and feeds them back to the company for immediate business adjustment. In the past, the industry generally did not attach great importance to the African market. But the analysis of the industry's big data in recent years shows him that there is actually potential demand in South Africa. After targeted marketing, South Africa now accounts for 8% of the company's business, an effective expansion of the company's sales channels.

In addition, the number of orders from Canada increased by 80% in the company's performance of nearly RMB 30 million exports in 2017, which is also the result of advanced layout based on big data analysis.

### The help of big data: branding operations of nobody-enterprises

When the growth of the company became steady, Sun began to attach importance to brand management. He believes that the factors including productivity, products, channels, and costs of CNC mechanic engraving equipment tend to be homogenized to a certain extent after years of development. Only through a branding operation can an enterprise, in the differentiated competition, have a deep impression on the buyers.

To increase the gold content of the brand, he hired the French international inspection bureau, which is well recognized by foreign customers, to carry out the certification and control of the company's quality system. The company was recognized as an honest company with fine quality. At the same time, it had also passed the national quality system certification ISO9001 and obtained the CE certification of EU countries and EU Free Trade Association national market.

As Sun made efforts in the direction of branding, an accident occurred disrupting the progress. Sun was unaware of the fact that a processing plant with which he had started cooperation as early as 2009 replaced key parts with fakes to lower the cost when producing a piece of equipment. After it was shipped abroad, it would not have broken down within 5 years except it did within half a year. When the buyer found out about the truth, he was infuriated. Sun promised to refund for the damaged goods and bear all the losses on his own.

Thereafter, he prioritized quality and decided to conduct the manufacturing himself. He set up his own factory. "It's mainly because after positioning the brand as selling medium-end and high-end products, I realized that the factories I used to partner with had different pursuits. They only see simple production but the importance of quality," helplessly complained Sun. Hard work enabled the company to grow to a scale where there are there are 33 employees. Once product quality is completely controlled, the rate for positive feedback increased. "The product can talk." Sun is confident to promise that to customers. In his opinion,

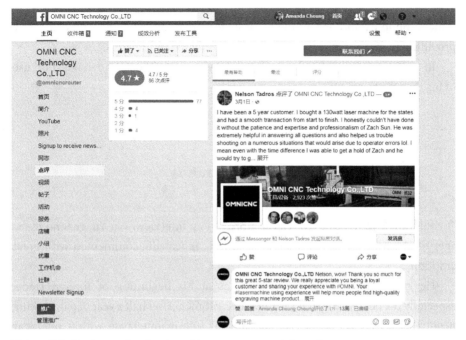

**Figure 5.2** Customer feedback on Sun company social media

the products by an enterprise are all conveying a sense of value that the enterprise cares about the brand. He hopes that when overseas customers mention his brand, they naturally associate it with fine quality.

A great advantage of Sun since he started his business is that he is good at embracing the Internet and adapting to the changes of the times. Since 2015, his company has also formed an unwritten strategic plan: all planning and layout follow the latest trends and changes in foreign trade in the Internet era. "Now the enterprises that perform well in foreign trade have grasped every change in the Internet era. Some don't realize that changes are constantly happening. They are hesitant to make a move. I often advise them to follow it, thus avoiding elimination by the times. "

In 1980, Alvin Toffler, a famous American futurist, predicted that big data would play a significant role in the future industrial revolution in The Third Wave. Alibaba began to arrange big data in 2010. With data precipitation, Alibaba provides scientific data analysis services for SMEs. Effectively, the information of suppliers and customers are matched to help suppliers with precision marketing. The extensive application of big data in marketing has completely changed the difficult blind exploration in the early stage of nobody-enterprises by constantly providing them with effective information guidance and reference.

In foreign trade 3.0, big data will weigh even more. Those who make good use of big data make profits.

\* \* \*

## Credit assistance

"I could not love the times of credit more." In an interview, Wu Yu, general manager of Shenyang Hyde Technology Co., Ltd., repeatedly commented with great emotion.

He clearly remembers the difficulties at his beginning of foreign trade, especially the deal with a South American customer. After half a year of painstaking negotiations over the deal, the warranty of free maintenance within one year put an end to it. The other party was not convinced: as a single round trip ticket from China to South America would cost RMB 20,000, how is a small company financially able to fulfill such a promise? They believed it was an empty promise. At last, they withdrew from the cooperation.

Wu's experience is nothing new to all SMEs in China. In particular, some sellers were willing to sell inferior and fake products to make more profits, which resulted in a trust crisis amongst foreign buyers of made-in-China products in the early years of China's economic globalization. Statistics show that every year, the Alibaba platform has up to US$20 billion deals that fail to close because of the distrust between both parties. In 2015, to solve the credit and trust issues of online transactions, Alibaba upgraded and transformed for another time from a single information display platform to a cross-border online trade platform. Cross-border B2B transactions with credit assurance came into being.

After the change of platform rules, Alibaba endorsed for small- and medium-sized foreign trade enterprises for their credit to global buyers via big data. The transactions are therefore vouched for, thus alleviating the credit doubts of foreign buyers and escorting SMEs to smoothly go global. Positively, many SMEs on the platform also seized the opportunity to establish enterprise credit and embark on the road of rapid development.

"I don't have contacts and resources offline, but I can make a difference online with convincing strength and credit," confidently expressed Wu, who successfully transformed from a teacher to an entrepreneur.

### Credit makes business

If not for a course of NC software operations, Wu, a nerd, might still be an ordinary teacher in the Mechanical Engineering Department of Shenyang Vocational and Technical College.

Wu entered the foreign trade circle by chance. In class, he learned that there is a kind of waterjet cutting machine technology different from traditional cutting. When water and abradant are mixed together, it can achieve high-speed jet at up to three times the speed of sound and cut metal, glass, ceramics, and non-metals. To better teach this course, Wu was sent to a factory for field research for two

**Figure 5.3** The three departments of production, design, and service of the company hold a meeting to solve the actual cutting problems encountered by customers

years. Upon his return, his great interest in the technology turned into efforts to improve it. In over a year, he designed a four-axis waterjet cutting machine and successfully patented it.

However, despite the advancement and fine quality of the machine, it was pricy, costing hundreds of thousands of RMB. Without any sales resources or channels, he decided to make full use of the Internet platform to open the market. In October 2011, Wu registered the membership at the Alibaba international station.

At the beginning, there were not many Chinese selling waterjet cutting machines online. As long as the basic information such as product photos, equipment parameters, prices, and after-sales services were uploaded, overseas customers would send inquiries upon searches. Three months later, the company received an order from Australia, which eased the stress on initial capital shortage. But as more peers entered the e-commerce platform, the difficulty of business escalated. At that time, his competitors were mainly from Nanjing. They were all traditional foreign trade enterprises that were deeply experienced in the industry for years. Some were powerful manufacturers, with 100,000 square meters of factory buildings alone. At that time, Wu's total capital was less than RMB 100,000, not to mention the absence of his own factory. The size of the processing factory with which he cooperated is also very small, only slightly over 1,000 square meters. If walking the traditional path of foreign trade with these competitors, Wu would have no competitive advantage.

The weakness also extended to the Internet. Wu was most impressed by the South American deal. After six months of contact, the buyer suddenly changed his mind at the last moment. The reason was that when it comes to after-sales service of the machine, Wu promised that the company's three after-sales engineers would provide a one-year warranty service. On the contrary, the promise raised suspicion for the other party whether the company would be financially capable to fulfill the promise to fly over and fix the product should it go wrong, since a round trip ticket from China to South America costs RMB 20,000. After considerations, the final decision was no deal.

Wu encountered similar situations more than once. For a long time, foreign trade transactions had to be handled by third-party intermediaries such as Singapore, due to the low trust of overseas buyers in Chinese suppliers. Later, even though cross-border e-commerce transactions have sprung up, a platform only displays product information. Thousands of miles away, foreign buyers would not easily put their faith in made-in-China products.

Despite Wu's confidence in the fine quality of the machine he designed, it is difficult to win the trust of the buyers. "I had nothing but credit, but no one believed it." Speaking of the past, Wu could not hide the sadness. And his predicament was not over until the Alibaba platform proposed a new solution.

## Small can go big

In 2015, similar distrust that happened to Wu was seen on Alibaba platform in large numbers. Alibaba upgraded and transformed once again by launching a cross-border B2B credit assurance system. It mainly evaluates the credit assurance limit, visualizes the transaction records, and digitalizes credit levels for users according to their authentic trade data, thus solving the mistrust between the

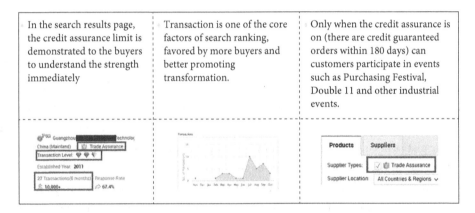

| In the search results page, the credit assurance limit is demonstrated to the buyers to understand the strength immediately | Transaction is one of the core factors of search ranking, favored by more buyers and better promoting transformation. | Only when the credit assurance is on (there are credit guaranteed orders within 180 days) can customers participate in events such as Purchasing Festival, Double 11 and other industrial events. |
|---|---|---|

**Figure 5.4** Illustration I of cross-border B2B credit assurance system

| The company information page displays transaction records, so that buyers can place orders more confidently | Credit assurance 1:1 accumulated transaction points upgrade the transaction level faster. | In the search results page, company business cards are displayed to show transaction level and highlight credibility. |
|---|---|---|

**Figure 5.5** Illustration II of cross-border B2B credit assurance system

**Figure 5.6** A product is explained to ensure that each component meets international standards

buyer and the seller in a transaction. With a credit endorsement from a platform as big as Alibaba, SMEs have demolished the credit barrier in online transactions.

Wu, who had been teaching computer science in college, is naturally sensitive to the changes in the Internet. When he was struggling for a way out for the company's development, he seized the opportunity making full use of the changes in the platform rules. "I don't have contacts and resources offline, but I can make a difference online with convincing strength and credit." Fully confident, he required the company to immediately apply credit assurance for all transactions. To actively promote the progress of new transaction channels, the company also rewarded RMB 500 to each salesman for each credit assured order completed. Agile and hardworking, Wu quickly accumulated excellent trading data.

Another bright spot in Alibaba's credit assurance system is the transparency of business transactions, which addresses the distrust of overseas buyers, therefore transactions are made efficiently. After this, the attitude of overseas buyers towards Chinese products underwent significant changes. Wu recalled that most of the efforts to seal a deal used to be on dispelling the credit doubts of the other party. It would take at least three months from the inquiry to sending samples for trial cutting, and to discussing transportation requirements and after-sales service. The credit assurance visualizes for buyers the credit level that Alibaba identifies for company. Directly, they would have an understanding and trust of the company's strength. Now, every order can be completed in 20 days on average. Once there was a Spanish customer who decisively made a payment seven days after the inquiry.

In the traditional method of foreign trade, many foreign buyers, concerned about the quality of the products, would fly to China for inspection in person. A great amount of money and energy were spent. But the implementation of the credit assurance system allows them to hire a third-party inspection company to check the goods, which also facilitates the transactions between the two parties.

In short, the launch of the credit assurance system enables overseas buyers to purchase made-in-China products at ease while China's export trade also welcomes new opportunities. Taking advantage of that, Wu's company grew rapidly: in 2016, the export volume doubled to US$1.5 million; in 2017, it increased to US$3 million; in 2018, the export volume in the first quarter alone exceeded US$1 million. Among them, the amount of transactions under the credit assurance system exceeded US$300,000, and the number of inquiries increased by 300% compared with the usual amount during the new trade festival held on Alibaba platform in March 2018.

### Intelligent manufacturing promotes credit upgrading

In the market of international trade, China has been only a substitute manufacturer for a long time, which is utterly at the bottom of the industrial chain. After stepping out of the predicament in the initial stage, many SMEs have realized that to truly eradicate the credit issues of overseas buyers, the quality of made-in-China products must be ensured and constantly improved; in addition, a reputation must be built to achieve brand production.

In retrospect, Wu entered the foreign trade industry by mistake with no capital, no contacts, and no factory buildings. His eyes were only on selling expensive machines without any awareness of branding at all. In 2015, when Alibaba's credit assurance system was newly launched, Wu's credit limit was not impressive, only over US$20,000. As the company grew rapidly and excellent platform transaction data accumulated, it has risen to nearly US$1 million, ranking first in the industry nationwide and exceeding the second by 50%. The achievement raised Wu's brand awareness. He began to focus on brand operations.

He found that the orders of waterjet cutting machines in traditional foreign trade were in large quantities, while small and personalized orders are the future trend of global development. But unfortunately, the equipment provided across the industry in the world is universal, which fails to meet the new needs of customers in the Internet era. He decided to position the company as a supplier of personalized customized cutting schemes, on top of which, a brand operation is performed. At the end of 2017, Wu signed a brand operation plan with a branding company to promote six waterjet cutting machines of different materials that he designed in the global market by further dividing the market and deeply targeting customers.

In the Internet era, new foreign trade will pay more attention to user experience. In this trend, a perfect after-sales service system of products is required to maintain enterprise credit. Exports of foreign waterjet cutting machines share the difficulty of rendering fine after-sales service. At present, Wu is trying to solve this problem with big data. He plans to install intelligent sensors inside each machine to capture the technical parameters such as abrasive consumption, water consumption, cutting speed, and pressure fluctuation at any time. In this way, the condition of each product across the world can be fed back to the company's backend database in real time. The company can judge the operation of the product immediately via monitoring and calculations and inform the customer in advance of potential risks. Wu said that once his attempt worked out, the company's products could be upgraded in the direction of automation and intelligence, thus taking the leap from made-in-China to intelligently-made-in-China.

Speaking of honesty, the rise of Dutch businessmen in the history of global trade deserves to be mentioned.

At the end of the 16th century, a Dutch merchant ship was trapped in the icy sea when it passed an island in Russia. The ship could not go on until the next year when the ice broke and melted. In addition to the captain, there were 17 sailors on the ship. Short of food and clothing, their lives were seriously threatened in the severe cold of 40 below zero. As long as the goods were opened, there would be clothes and medicines they urgently needed. But everyone on board agreed that it was the goods entrusted by the customers and they could not open them.

In the icy days, the captain led the sailors to live by hunting, during which eight died, one after another. Eight months later, when the surviving sailors delivered the intact goods to the clients, entire Europe was overwhelmed by their integrity. Since then, customers have flocked to Holland, which has won precious trust, laying an important foundation for the rise of the country in modern times.

Since ancient times, Chinese valued integrity, and the idiom 一诺千金 (a promise is worth a thousand pieces of gold) came into use from the ancient book *Records of the Historian*. In the Internet era, the rise of cross-border B2B credit assured transactions will naturally eliminate dishonest businesses while honest SMEs share the dividend of the times. This is the process that a promise is turned to gold.

What's more, the credit assurance system breaks the tradition and establishes a new set of evaluation rules. All large- and medium-sized enterprises participating in international competition have equal opportunities. The fertile new commercial landscape gave rise to the vigorous development of thousands of honest and adventurous SMEs.

\* \* \*

## Management innovation

Xu Dan, aged 33, the general manager of Nantong Roke Fluid Equipment Co., Ltd., is definitely a dark horse in the foreign trade circle. In just two years, the company has made many achievements: in 2016, orders increased by 305% and in 2017, by 380%. The team he led also set a record of the fastest order seal time of 2 hours and 20 minutes.

Xu, fierce and tall, has the nickname Super Dan in foreign trade circles. In fact, he has made steady progress one step at a time. After graduating from university, he was employed at a foreign company as an ordinary junior employee. Gradually, he was promoted to be the purchasing director of a large foreign manufacturing enterprise. In 2016, Xu, who likes challenges, chose to start his business in the machining industry, with which he was completely unfamiliar. Compared with the previous employer, his venture partner company was not large in scale and economic strength. Taking the new job, Xu did not rush to implement changes, but studied the history of China's foreign trade first. A careful analysis of the industry changes in the past five to ten years led him to make a major adjustment on the company's development path, from the original single offline transaction to mainly marketing on various e-commerce platforms.

Xu also found that machining has matured in China. In the past few decades, the process has not greatly changed, meaning little room for innovation in products. What is left to do is to make bold innovations in enterprise management to re-stimulate the vitality of factories and suppliers. This is the only way to make it happen, that the latecomers surpass the old-timers.

### *New model 1: the consortium grows and succeeds together*

In 2015, to motivate mutual progress and share resources, Xu's partners and the head of two other foreign trade companies worked together in an industrial park in Nantong and established an e-commerce school to train talents.

The core of the Internet era is to share. After joining the entrepreneurial team, Xu found the joint office mode was effective and decided to make it something. On top on the original mode, he created joint recruitment, joint training, joint Player Kill (PK, or internal competition), and unified operation to form a joint office management mode. This consortium mode is also an innovation in the foreign trade management team of domestic SMEs.

In the joint office mode, Xu pays most attention to enterprise talent training. In particular in unified operation, the original separate personnel layout of each company will be broken in the consortium but all employees are integrated into a unified management. Then, they are divided into different training sections according to their strong suits to maximize the talent advantages of the team. For example, if some salesmen are good at platform marketing, they are assigned to train others in platform marketing; if some salesmen are very familiar with the website and social platforms, they are responsible for training others the application and operation of the network platforms. In this way, the advantage of talents in the consortium can be maximized so that each company has diverse talents, which therefore improves the business capacity of the company.

Apart from the identity as founder, Xu has injected the corporate culture gene of sharing into the company. A crucial assessment basis for the promotion of salesman to supervisor and supervisor to senior manager is the willingness and ability to help others. Xu explains that if whoever is reluctant to help others, share his/her own successful experiences, or put himself/herself in other's shoes can't lead a team or become a manager.

When the consortium was founded, only three companies joined. In 2016, Xu's takeover increased the number to five. In that year, the integration of resources in the consortium resulted in growth in performance of each company with the smallest one up by over 50%. In 2017, the number grew to 12; the performance growth was even greater with an average of 100% to 200%; all of the members ranked among the top 10 in the industry.

### New mode 2: Spare no cost to cultivate the post-90s generation

According to Alibaba platform's latest buyer portrait, the average age of overseas buyers is 39, of which 31% are between 25 and 34 years old. They prefer to deal with foreign trade affairs by means of mobile phones, instant messaging, and Internet connections. Those born in the 90s in China are generally recognized as the generation most familiar with the Internet and best at Internet thinking. Xu believes that the number of staff born in the 90s that foreign trade enterprises train can largely determine whether enterprises can seize new business opportunities first.

Xu, once a foreign company's procurement manager, has a deep understanding of the buyer's psychology. As early as 2016, he rearranged the company's development framework from a buyer's perspective by establishing a new sales center, where all salesmen are required to negotiate based on improving a buyer's experience. At employee training, the focus was on the how a buyer thinks, what he/she wants, and what he/she worries about. Consequently, the buyer's trust and inquiry transaction probability are increased.

Different from the traditional master-apprentice training of old salesmen in many foreign trade companies, Xu's consortium very willing to spare no cost on personnel training. From recruitment to formal onboarding, the talent reserve period lasts four months, including one month of training and three months of probation. On average, the total training cost per employee is as high as RMB 10,000.

In foreign trade, there is frequent turnover of salesmen. Many bosses are worried that salesmen will switch jobs as they mature in the business. Why does Xu have to go the opposite way and invest that much in talent training? Xu explains that he studied the psychological characteristics of job seekers born in the 90s, who are totally different from those born in the 70s and 80s. What they care about most are whether the company has a prospect, whether there is much to learn, and whether their self-worth is recognized and achieved. Income is no longer the determining factor. Therefore, Xu's targeted business training is very popular among employees born in the 90s and the talent team has been relatively stable with a turnover rate controlled under 15%.

In addition, Xu did the math. For example, suppose a company hires 10 new employees in two years. Even if only one salesperson stays, he/she is able to bring nearly RMB 200,000 of economic benefit in one year. Despite the early cost of training, the company gains profit instead of losing investment, because once the trained salesperson goes into foreign trade practice, his/her trained capability will pay off. In 2016 and 2017, the business growth of Xu's company exceeded 300%, among which the contribution of new employees accounted for 45% and 55% respectively. Some employees even independently completed a transaction only four days after coming onboard.

### New mode 3: The large trade of small factories

In present foreign trade, there are more and more small and micro overseas buyers as well as more and more fragmented orders. Some customers may only ask for 100 products in one deal. Faced with these fragmented orders, many foreign trade companies are particularly worried as the traditional substitute manufacturing factories are more willing to perform mass production. Xu's factory is not large, with only 37 employees and nearly 70% of the products are made by suppliers. The dependence on them is quite strong. But it's strange that no matter how small an order is, the suppliers agree to produce without hesitation. What's the key behind this?

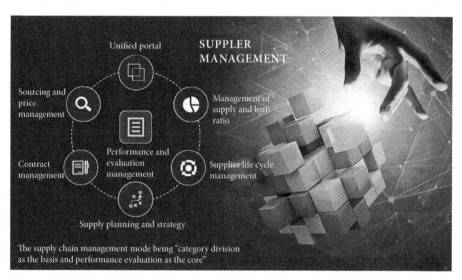

**Figure 5.7** Xu's supplier management system

Xu discloses that it is the utter change of cooperative thinking pattern with suppliers that pulls the trick. In the past, many foreign trade companies saw themselves as superior to suppliers because they believed that suppliers depended heavily on them to profit, thus naturally prioritizing their needs. In fact, this kind of cooperation is not equal, nor can it last. Therefore, Xu applies the concept of resource integration, as when he built the consortium. A business model of large trade for small factories was therefore created. He upgraded the relationship between himself and the suppliers to a strategic partnership, extended the enterprise management directly to the upstream supply chain, and created a new type of cooperation that can flexibly adjust production at any time in response to the changes of the Internet era.

Xu's management of suppliers consists of six parts: source search, price management, contract management, performance assessment, supplier life cycle management, and supply proportion management. He explained that the concept of large trade for small factories actually took the unique advantage of the development of made-in-China products as of today. After 40 years of reform and opening up, the production of many substitute manufacturing factories in China has reached their best level across the world, where the quality is excellent and the cost incredibly low. Xu decided to take the advantage of flexible scheduling and distribution. For example, if a product requires six processes, traditional production would assign all to one factory. Now, he divides the six processes to six factories. Each handles the part it is best at, while the final assembly is performed in his own plant, where the logo of his brand is labelled. In this way, quality is further improved and cost reduced.

Xu is bold and meticulous. In the whole production process, he will send team members carefully trained by the company to participate in management to help the other party improve productivity and process. The intervention can have the production cycle of a supplier shortened from 30 days to 20 and the qualification rate increased from 95% to 99.5%. Suppliers would naturally not say no to such win-win cooperation

Before Xu started his business in 2015, the export volume of his partners was only US$350,000. After a series of distribution, the company started to make a breakthrough: in 2016, the orders increased by 305%, and in 2017, by more than 380%, with the export volume reaching US$5.81 million.

Summing up this successful experience, Xu emphasizes the corresponding change of thinking patterns behind the change of management mode. He concludes that the traditional foreign trade sells whatever products the factory produces as a substitute manufacturer, which is totally based on the position and thinking of the seller. In the Internet age, the buyer's mentality and groups have changed greatly. We must change our thinking patterns to understand what foreign buyers ask for and worry about and then carry out the company's top-level design according to their needs.

In Xu's top-level design management plan, the core idea is to nurture talents. Directed at new employees, the methods of joint recruitment, joint training, joint PK, and unified operations are adopted to integrate the human resources of different companies to form a shared corporate culture and improve the overall competitiveness. Regarding the newly hired born in the 90, their spiritual needs for growth are respected and met. In the four-month training, the fittest survive after rounds of elimination and selection. For suppliers, the concept of large foreign trade for small factories is proposed, upgrading a simple cooperative relationship to strategic partnership, so as to grow together and for mutual benefit in win-win situations. More importantly, this new type of cooperation is particularly suitable for the current trend of small and fragmented foreign trade, so Xu can focus on expanding territory in the new business environment.

"The core of enterprise management is the head, whose ideas matter the most," is how Xu summed up the secret of becoming Super Dan.

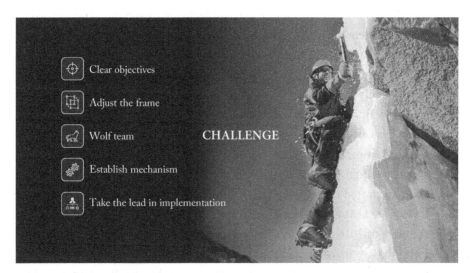

**Figure 5.8** Xu's mode

Take a closer look at the path of the rise of the nobody foreign trade enterprises in the Internet era, it can be noticed that all of them actively adapt to the changes of the times and seize the opportunities in industrial transformation. Especially in the process of the young Xu's strong rise in a short period, his insight, decisiveness, and courage to embrace changes are what many traditional small- and medium-sized enterprise owners lack. Also, Wu spent a lot of time on study every year. He has repeatedly stressed that despite the experience as a computer science teacher in college before starting his own business and better Internet thinking patterns among those born in the 70s, he has to keep learning and stay vigilant in case of elimination in the rapid developments.

No matter how advanced the ideas of the management are, turning them into practice is the real deal. The thinking height of management determines the height of enterprise development. In all the fast-growing SMEs, managers are good at cultivating teams and injecting their ideas into the company's daily organization. They also carry out regular training for the professional knowledge of employees, share experiences among teams with nothing reserved, conduct professional management of suppliers, and pay attention to the building of organizational culture and team culture. All of these support the overall improvement of an enterprise's soft power.

In terms of products, the new generation of small- and medium-sized enterprise managers are determined to change the stereotyped image of made-in-China commodities, attach importance to quality, establish a fine international credit, and reshape the image of made-in-China products internationally through their practical efforts.

From starting from scratch to becoming an elite in the industry, China's nobody SMEs are making great achievements in the world foreign trade arena with the help of the Internet platform.

# CHAPTER VI

# New Chinese Suppliers Going Abroad

I N LONDON, ISTANBUL, OR Cape Town, when a young overseas seller logs in to the Alibaba platform on his/her mobile phone, he/she intends to find high-quality suppliers and new products in the shortest time and hopes to get fixed services. For example, when he/she gets off work, the order starts to be produced as promised in China; this is the new scene of foreign trade purchasing since 2017 across the globe.

This year, the overall cross-border trade market trend witnessed significant changes. As mentioned before, from commodity shortage to commodity surplus, the market experienced the gradual shift from a seller's market to a buyer's market. In the new round of statistics of overseas buyers, the proportion of retailers and wholesalers was as high as 46%, showing a new trend of small-B-type buyers (annual purchase amount less than US $500,000), big-B-type order fragmentation, etc.

In 2017, the Alibaba platform, in line with the new trends of foreign trade, again made a significant upgrade and adjustment. Starting from the buyer experience, it launched "fine business, fine products, and fine services" to promote the change of Chinese suppliers from made-in-China to China Made with a fine reputation in the global market.

\* \* \*

## Fine business (I)

"What award? The Golden Bull award?" On a normal working day in April 2018, Wang Jiejun, general manager of Qingdao Century Import and Export Co., Ltd. (hereinafter referred to as Century), was occupied with meetings as usual. During a meeting, he received a phone call, where Alibaba's Qingdao regional general manager broke the news to him that he was rated as one of the top 10 fine businesses of the first Golden Bull award.

Fine business is Alibaba's new direction to improve the overall competence of Chinese suppliers, which refers to high-quality suppliers that have strong e-commerce service capacity, R & D and design capacity, production and manufacturing capacity, and service awareness, therefore leading the foreign trade industry on the international station. The Golden Bull award is the highest honor Alibaba sets for SMEs. Wang is the only winner of the Golden Bull award among 130,000 Chinese suppliers engaged in cross-border e-commerce transactions on the international station platform.

**Figure 6.1** A Golden Bull moment

## *Transformation to e-commerce operation and breakthrough in enterprise development*

Century was founded in 2008, an untimely year. Soon after the start-up, the financial crisis struck and the orders volume dropped sharply. Helpless, Wang began to attend exhibitions like a traditional foreign trader. In March 2009, when he showed up with samples at the Chicago exhibition, he found that a third of the exhibition hall was closed. "My head went blank. What should I do?" Years later, Wang still remembers the helplessness as he stood in the empty exhibition site. He decided immediately to change the traditional mode of foreign trade; not to take orders passively from existing customers, but to open up new channels to actively look for orders.

In June 2009, as the global economy began to recover, overseas orders came back. At this turn, Wang stayed alert for crisis. He made profound changes inside Century. His own direct sales website was set up, a professional photography team was assembled to collect product materials, pictures of a product were required to be taken from five angles on the standard area. For some time, these actions made him appear to be a weirdo among peers.

In 2010, Wang became a member of the Alibaba platform. The entry benefited him with a profound judgment on the foreign trade situation: the market share of traditional foreign trade was declining year by year, but the emerging cross-border e-commerce had a good momentum, therefore more effort should be on e-commerce operations.

At that time, many foreign trade companies adopted the approach that a sales-man was multitasked for inquiry, documentation, and e-commerce operations. Wang believed that it would divide the salesman's attention and have none done well. So he took a bold move to establish a special e-commerce department and recruit full-time e-commerce operators. This department plays the role of a watch-tower in the company, conducting market predictions and activities operations through big data collection and analysis. Once a new product is launched at the initial stage, the company quickly locates and breaks into the target market by market share estimation, advertising, and visual marketing. Salesmen play the role of a propellant. They have to better understand the market and customer needs to better serve customers. In his view, only when both roles are well played can the march forward be steadier.

"Every time we finish decorating an Ali shop, there are always some competitors who make imitations and even infringe our brand for their own promotion. But they never defeat us." Wang explains that the secret is to leave professional tasks to the professionals; naturally the results will be doubled with half the effort.

Wang attaches great importance to the information display of products. His professional e-commerce team keeps the fighting spirit in practice. At the 2018 new trade festival, when the international station demanded each company to submit three videos, Century unexpectedly provided 100 videos from different angles for selection.

### Pay attention to the user needs and make personalized products

In June 2013, Wang attended an exhibition in Orlando. At that time, Century had built a good reputation in the global market, so he spared no cost to make the most luxurious booth among Chinese exhibitors. "This sends the message to customers all over the world that as foreign peers, Chinese are fully capable of making the products with the best quality in the world."

**Figure 6.2** The unique exhibition culture of Century

When Wang went to inspect the booth on the day prior to the exhibition opening, he found that the product display effect was different from what he expected. Originally, white natural marble products were supposed to go with cold lighting, but warm lighting was used, which resulted in poor visual presentation. Wang is a perfectionist in product details. He immediately decided to replace it with cold lights, which were often available. Unfortunately, he drove over to the supermarket near the exhibition and found none. Many supermarkets explained there was not enough inventory and it would take a week to transfer the goods. In the end, he had to buy the lights from the exhibition party at an insanely high price of $10,000 per light to get the visual effect that he was content with.

Wang learned a great deal from this incident. He found that conventional orders were decreasing and more customers began to have personalized needs and process requirements: "I sense a change of trends in the market are brewing." On the flight back from the United States, he decided to set up his own product design and development studio and independent factory to provide personalized and fine product services.

Later, the change of global foreign trade trends proved his sharp judgment correct. It is precisely the product design and product process and new manufacturing oriented to market demand that enabled the company to grow into a company with fine business on the Alibaba platform. "The essence of business is products. Customers want the products they need whether on Alibaba platform or other platforms." Wang said that good customer experience, first of all, was better efficiency to find products they want, so a platform like Alibaba is necessary; what suppliers need to do is to let customers see the company's products first after understanding the operation mechanism of the platform. But more importantly, efficient understanding and meeting of customer needs is to achieve a good customer experience.

Behind the personalized demand, higher requirements were put forward for product development and innovation. Century's customers include the world's most well-known supermarkets and industry purchasers. To meet the demand of purchasers for innovative products every year, there are more than 100 appearance patents of Mosaic products in Century's independent design studio alone.

"As a foreign trader, we have gone through a lot in the past two or three years, suffering the difficulties and transformation of foreign trade." Wang confessed that for a long time in the past, Chinese suppliers were merely copying overseas model.

Except that the international trade situation has changed, more overseas buyers are using WeChat to communicate with Chinese suppliers and the Alibaba platform to obtain business opportunities and seal deals. They show more willingness to come to China for in-depth exchanges.

On the day when he received the Golden Bull award in Hangzhou, Wang met nine other winners from various fields such as 1688 Retail and Rural Taobao. As they stood on the stage receiving thunderous applause, it was no longer a simple commendation to the leaders of fine business, but an affirmation of their successful business models. This is a new start for China: the strategy of going abroad.

\* \* \*

## Fine Business (II)

In February 2017, Qu Huijing, who was born in the 80s, began to use the Alibaba platform for foreign trade entrepreneurship. In just one year, it became one of the fastest growing small- and medium-sized SMEs in Jining City, Shandong Province. The average order-forming time in the machinery industry being about six months, she landed the first order in less than one month; with costs being recovered in one year on average, she made profits in half a year. The sales volume of the company in 2017 was RMB eight million, and the orders in the first three months alone increased by 1000% year-on-year in 2018. It is expected that the annual sales volume will achieve a new growth milestone.

On the Internet platform, foreign trade companies generally advocate wolf culture, but Qu's company is relatively casual. Without a special situation, there is no difference between the company's schedule and domestic trade enterprises. The working hours are from 8:30 A.M to 5:30 P.M. "Overtime is not recommended on weekends," she laughed. Qu had had simple work experience before. After college graduation, she worked as a white-collar employee in a Taiwan-funded enterprise in Shenzhen. In 2014, she returned to her hometown of Jining, Shandong Province, and worked as a foreign trade director in a mechanical manufacturing company until 2017, when she started her own business. It was the year with the advent of new opportunities for cross-border e-commerce development. Diligent, positive, and aggressive, she resolutely seized the opportunity to grow into a three-star fine business on Alibaba platform.

*Fine business: Information display should focus on the buyer experience*

Three-star fine business refers to businesses on the Alibaba international station that have strong e-commerce service capacity, R & D and design capacity, production and manufacturing capacity, and service awareness, therefore leading the foreign trade industry.

In 2017, Alibaba international station's overseas buyers showed a series of new trends. Their sourcing habits changed, with 70% of overseas buyers looking for business by products. The change required a seller to display product information from the perspective of buyer experience and make timely adjustments from the perspective of the information display. This is an important reason why Qu's e-commerce service capacity was strong enough to transform her from an ordinary entrepreneur to a fine one.

However, at the beginning of foreign trade, Qu didn't pay attention to the buyer experience but how to attract overseas buyers visually. And the visual evaluation standard was totally subjective: pictures were uploaded casually, some being mechanical equipment on the assembly line or in the workshop, and some waiting for shipment at the dock. To make the pictures eye-catching, she also outlined them with a bold red border and displayed as much product quality information such as EU certification as possible. Qu's product photos for display were informative without a trace of beauty.

As Alibaba grasped the new changes in the purchasing habits of overseas buyers in the second half of 2017, it timely revised the rules of product release

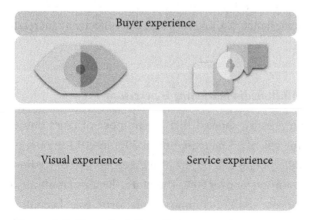

**Figure 6.3** Characteristics of buyer experience

**Figure 6.4** A Qu company Poster on the Ali store

on the platform, requiring stores to focus on buyer experience by optimizing the unified image style and presenting the visual effect of serious sellers and goods. "I was enlightened instantly." Qu confessed that she suddenly realized that all kinds of unprofessional display of information could easily leave overseas buyers an impression that made-in-China is cheap. She modified all the photos at once.

It was massive amount of work because she displayed more than 6,000 products on the platform. Only 3,000 products remained with more explicit information after screening. Among the 3,000 products, each has six pictures for display. Therefore, all staff were required to learn Photoshop, for which the company made an exception to impose overtime. It took only one day to reprocess nearly 20,000 pictures. Finally, it presented a clean and clear display, which improved buyers' visual experience during browsing, thus effectively increasing the inquiry conversion rate.

### Fine business: Multimedia marketing is necessary

The Alibaba survey also showed that the number of cross-border e-commerce buyers under the age of 35 increased from 30% in 2014 to 60% in 2017 and the number of mobile-phone-end buyers also exceeded that of traditional computer-end buyers, accounting for over 50%. Therefore, the use of multimedia information on the cross-border B2B e-commerce platform was becoming increasingly important in terms of the purchase habits of young buyers. In addition to video, they are also fond of new media forms such as AR, VR, and 360 panoramic display. These new media technologies can help them understand suppliers and commodities faster and more comprehensively by narrowing the gap caused by time and distance. Similarly, suppliers can successfully attract buyers' attention by rich and diverse multimedia information displays.

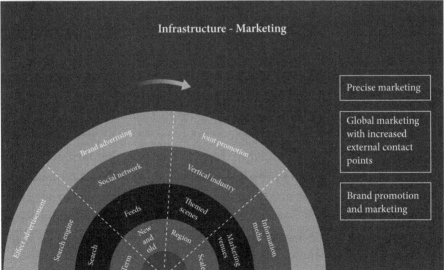

**Figure 6.5** Illustration of multimedia marketing at Alibaba.com

In the change of buyer's purchasing habits, it is necessary for cross-border e-commerce platforms to provide the support of full content manufacturing chain to help suppliers quickly acquire multimedia marketing capability and adapt to the change of buyer's new demands for information display. Since 2018, the Alibaba platform has started to enable a multimedia display of information and encourage suppliers to upload video, animation, panorama, and other forms of content. At present, the number of businesses using video to display products on the platform has reached 57,000, and the number of products with video introduction to overseas buyers has exceeded 5.2 million.

In this regard, Qu is a pioneer. As early as the beginning of her business, she realized the importance of using video display when receiving inquiries from buyers. She asked all saleswomen of the team to learn simple operations of mechanical equipment and recorded them a 40-second video that gives an introduction of the equipment, which was sent to overseas buyers during online chats or email exchanges. The communicative effect turned out to be positive: first, the product introduction which used to take about 10 minutes is done in a short video; second, that young saleswomen can operate large machinery sends a message that the equipment is easy to operate. A New Zealand customer saw the video of wood digger operating sent by the salesman, made no further bargain, and paid a deposit within a week.

Following the upgrading of the Alibaba international station in 2018, Qu also optimized and repositioned the video content. The mechanical equipment operation videos have been changed to use engineers wearing a uniform, whose operation action is more professional, giving a new impression of a rigorous enterprise. When communicating offline or exchanging email with a buyer, videos of the saleswomen operating the mechanical equipment continued to be used.

Qu predicted that the development trend of cross-border e-commerce in the future would be that buyers can make positive and negative comments on the Alibaba platform as they do on Taobao shopping, therefore allowing fine business to stand out. Since the end of 2017, she has actively encouraged customers to leave comments upon order acceptance. For the machinery and equipment export industry, an order from the payment of deposit to the equipment shipped across the sea to customers, will take three months to complete, thus the difficulty to get positive reviews, but there are buyers who have left her valuable five-star reviews.

### *Active adjustment for the company according to the new trend*

In March 2018, the new trade festival on the Alibaba platform set off a foreign trade carnival around the world. Qu's company performed well, with daily visitors increasing from the usual 300 to 2,000, who made 26 inquiries on average every day. Throughout the festival, online and offline sales reached US$220,000. As soon as the festival ended, she timely and proactively rearranged the company's overall marketing in 2018 according to the new trend disclosed in big data analysis.

The company discovered a large number of potential customers in the new trade festival. She required the salesmen to classify them, strengthen the follow-up communication through phone calls and emails, and strive to transform them into real customers as much as possible.

In addition, the new trend shows that there are more customers from Europe and America with the increasing influence of Alibaba platform despite the fact that Southeast Asian customers used to be the majority, accounting for over 30% of the company. But the European and American customers are different from those in Southeast Asia. They have higher and more precise requirements for products. For example, EU customers require the products to have CE certificate, and the American customers demand the engines of mechanical equipment to be EPA certified.

Qu adjusted the company's marketing strategy again. First of all, the order of product display was rearranged. Products with CE certificate and EPA certificate are all promoted on the front page of the webstore, and the use of video introductions were also significantly increased. The second is to actively enhance product quality, which increases the purchase cost by 10%. In terms of production, more strict quality requirements were implemented. As a result, the quality of all products in the company has been improved the price remaining unchanged, which has become a selling point in Qu's subsequent company publicity.

Qu's machinery and equipment for the European and American markets have also been put into the Southeast Asian market. Many people are wondering why upgrade the products now that the Southeast Asian market is doing fine. "Fine quality is the key to business lasting longer," she explained. Facts have proved her correct. After the product was updated, its market share went up in Southeast Asia. Many customers who received the samples changed their order from a couple of pieces of equipment to a couple of containers of equipment.

### *Use Internet rules to build a team*

Qu's company, as Alibaba's demonstration base, receives visits from many Jining enterprises for learning. She noticed that the most common question was how to build a team. Some bosses, who believe that the more salesmen are recruited, the more orders will be brought in, and blindly expand the company's scale. As a result, with human resource costs being high, the operation of the company experienced no improvement at all. The skillful use of Internet rules to complete team building and management and effectively improve team cohesion is also one of the important reasons why Qu has built fine business in a short time with only a few salesmen.

When Qu started foreign trade, like many, she didn't know how to manage or build a team. After she hired the first salesman, she started the business in a hurry. Later, as the company's development got on track, she recruited a few more salespeople. But problems soon surfaced. Qu found that they were all immersed in their orders. As the head, she did not know how to manage them. "I don't know what they really think, and it's difficult to have them united as a team."

Fortunately, Qu is a persistent thinker familiar with various trading rules of cross-border e-commerce platforms. She decided to set up the team operation

**Figure 6.6** An Alibaba activity for Jining Enterprises

according to the rules of Alibaba platform. There were five sub accounts affiliated to one master account for a team leader and five salesmen, her first team. On the platform, there is a clear division between the master account and the sub accounts. Qu assigned a supervisor to take charge of the master account and the salespeople to take charge of the sub accounts. The supervisor focused on the operation while the salespeople assisted in the management and supervision. As a result, team management was efficient and clear. Qu revealed that this was the reason why the company could recover the investment cost in one-half year. "When the foundation of a team is stable, the company will operate normally. Otherwise without a team, the platform alone is not enough."

After combing Qu's entrepreneurial experience, it can be found that she has taken steady and flexible steps in the whole process. Especially, she excels at seizing the new opportunities of cross-border e-commerce development, adjusting her own marketing strategy and the company's operation layout in time, and presenting information from the perspective of the buyer experience; she also has strong multi-media operations and marketing capability, which has borne fruit in positive results before the new trends. Then, she applied new media marketing in a more accurate and professional manner. In terms of team building, her method appears to be commonplace, except it is not. The existing rules of the Internet platform were transplanted to her company, which was then managed according to the characteristics of employees in practice. This has built a solid foundation for the rapid development of the company.

Qu is hardworking, open-minded, willing to share, and aggressive. As every step was taken steadily, she seized the opportunities decisively as soon as they came and quickly grew into a three-star fine business on the Alibaba platform.

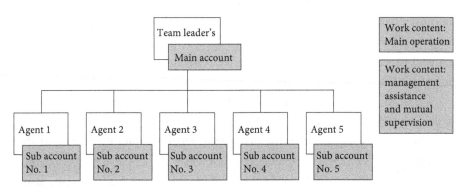

**Figure 6.7** Qu company team building

\* \* \*

## Fine products

Whoever walks into Harvest SPF Textile (Beijing) Co., Ltd. (hereinafter referred to as Harvest) will be attracted by two cabinets full of the patent certificates and trademark registration certificates. "We have registered over 20 invention patents, utility model patents, and over 10 new material brands. Many awards were won, but most of them have not been retained," humbly explained Liang Xiaofeng, one of the founders.

Liang and her husband Xu Dong, as college graduates in the early 1980s, were bold and restless. They have accurately stepped right on the node of the development of the times in every decisive choice in their lives, from giving up stable and superior work in the system to going into business and creating their own patented products, and to becoming a three-star fine product supplier on the Alibaba platform in the Internet age.

### *Fine product: start with high professional sensitivity*

Fine product is a new initiative put forward by the Alibaba platform for serious products according to the new trend of the foreign trade industry in recent years. As the name suggests, suppliers are supposed to develop and design products with their own patents that are on the cutting-edge in industry.

It was a long journey for Liang and Xu from starting their own business to making fine products. After graduating from the university in 1983, they both became reporters for a news agency in Beijing. In 1992, there was a wave of starting one's own business in China. The next year, Xu, inspired by the times, decided to resign and join the wave. He first printed flight schedules for CAAC, then made gift packages for famous foreign enterprises in Beijing, and also ran a government information kiosk, which was seen as a very advanced concept at that time.

Seeing Xu exploring in business, Liang also paid attention to opportunities to switch jobs. While studying at the People's Daily News seminar, she came across that China was going to open the first public relations training course. At that time, the world's top 500 companies began to enter the Chinese market in force. But the public relations field was still a blank slate at home. Liang realized that a huge opportunity was being presented in front of her. After completing the PR training course in her spare time, she resolutely jumped to the first PR company established in China and became a witness to major economic events such as Coca Cola's reentering China and McDonald's first store opening in Beijing. Later, Liang jumped ship to an internationally renowned sports promotion company to participate in the bid of the Chinese government for the 2008 Olympic Games, while introducing major international events such as golf, tennis, and F1 into China. With the take-off of China's economy in the 1990s, Liang saw many Chinese enterprises grow step by step from small workshops. As a senior manager of the company, she felt the urge to start her entrepreneurship.

In 2001, when Liang, 40 years old, was planning a press conference for Li Guanqi, the father of soybean protein fiber, she discovered a business opportunity and started her own business in the completely strange textile industry. Her journey to make fine products thus began.

### Several life-and-deaths for the company

Liang majored in metals and non-metals. It was not until entering a completely new textile industry with blind passion that she tasted the real difficulties. At that time, although the world-shocking soybean protein fiber material was invented, subsequent spinning, weaving, and dyeing technologies were a complete zero. Every step was a blind exploration. Once, the company lost RMB 500,000 due to the lack of knowledge about soybean protein fiber's poor resistance to high temperature. They chose to experiment, improve, and produce together. As a result, the over RMB five million investment was soon gone.

Just when Harvest was about become bankrupt, a well-known domestic company volunteered for cooperation. When Xu basically mastered the characteristics and weaknesses of soybean protein fiber, the two parties signed a contract of over RMB 20 million. Unexpectedly there were many problems in the production again. In the final accounting, there was RMB one million lost, without any profit at all.

Harvest spent the first five years in great difficulty until a Russian businessman came via the company's official website asking them to make a series of products with angora (rabbit hair). The couple decided to try for the last time. Half a year later, the Russian customers were satisfied with the finished sample and

**Figure 6.8** The company participated in the Alibaba purchase launch ceremony as a representative of fine business

immediately placed an order of over US $1 million. The company came back from the edge of collapse. The sudden Russian buyer made them realize the great value of Internet platform in foreign trade.

In 2008, Harvest became a member of the Alibaba international station and soon attracted its attention. The station regularly invited it to participate in various business training and teaches them new functions immediately. Harvest's e-commerce operation has been improved rapidly as a result. It has become one of the few three-star suppliers on the platform. Thanks to Alibaba's promotion, Harvest's new materials are known to more overseas buyers. The inquiry is spot-on and its conversion rate has always been maintained over 40%. Especially after the launch of Alibaba's credit assurance system, export business of conventional channels has become simple and convenient, greatly improving the speed of order placement. This is in line with the current new trend of small-batch multi-frequency foreign trade.

### Independent R & D + marketing, a leading business model

In 2012, Liang and her husband discovered another huge business opportunity on the Internet.

At that time, some people in South Korea harnessed the antibacterial nature of copper to produce copper fiber. In this technology, liquid copper is sprayed on the surface of the fiber in the production, but copper is both easy to fall off and costly. Xu decided to improve the production process of copper fiber after discovering this new material with great market potential. In trails and errors, copper was chelated on the chemical bond of the fiber and a new type of copper fiber was developed.

Copper fiber attracted the attention of a British customer after it was launched on the e-commerce platform. Upon receiving the samples, the British customer took the fabric to the Microbial Laboratory of Southampton University in England for testing, and the test results came out surprising. The copper fiber fabric not only has an over 99.9% antibacterial rate against common bacteria, but also an excellent antibacterial effect on the virulent pathogenic bacteria MRSA. Therefore, he asked Harvest to develop over 20 kinds of products. Later, these products received a good response in the United Kingdom and the United States. In just a few years, the market share of copper fiber products has developed from a few samples to millions of dollars of overseas purchases per annum.

The advent of copper fiber products made Harvest famous while encouraging the transformation of some traditional foreign companies. At that time, the fourth biggest phone card company in the United States took the initiative to contact Harvest on Alibaba platform. The head of that company told Liang that the popularity of mobile phones has a massive impact on their traditional phone card business. The company's production volume was shrinking rapidly. They had no intention being a sitting duck. Instead, they were planning to open up new markets. And as soon as they discover the copper fiber fabric produced by Harvest, they immediately placed an order of compression socks production made of copper fiber yarn using the antibacterial and deodorizing nature of the fabric. The launch of the product also received a positive response in the U.S. market. This phone card company made a successful transformation thanks to these compression socks.

The test results of copper fiber materials at Southampton University and the recognition of overseas market greatly encouraged the couple to apply for their first invention patent. Thereafter, there have been a growing number of invention patents and utility model patents. Then, having drawn lessons from the hardships on independent investment in R & D in the early stage of the business start-up, Harvest adopted the smile-curve mode of by grasping the market frontier dynamics and trends and interacting with customers on product demand instead.

First, efforts are invested in the R & D of patented technology and the protection of intellectual property rights; second is in the promotion of the international market. Market demand drives the integration and production of the production chain, which reduces the R & D expenditure and speeds up the transformation cycle from patent to product.

### Patent as a shield in frequent trade wars

Good at discovering various business opportunities in the transformation of the times, Liang was also extremely accurate in identifying changes in overseas markets. In the past two years, she found that the orders for new fabrics have decreased from 100,000 pieces to thousands. As the clothing update for younger generation accelerates, some orders are as small as 1,000 pieces and 500. The trend of miniaturization becomes increasingly common. The market demand for new products keeps growing. In this case, a supplier should go beyond passively making products that meet the needs of the buyer to actively developing new products that lead the trend, so as to remain in the leading position.

The R & D experience accumulated over the years has also enabled Harvest to cope with the new changes in the foreign trade environment with ease. They have developed more than ten utility model patents, many of which are new products developed and designed in line with the needs of buyers. For example, when some customers feedback said that the socks were uncomfortable to wear, they designed an open compression sock; there were also shoes and socks suitable for the gym. Wearing them for whether fitness or yoga no longer requires sneakers.

It was in the R & D of new products that they found that whether at home or abroad more people go to the gym, thus predicted that the future global trend of new textile materials industry is towards the development of health wear. They began to lay it out in advance. In recent years, their R & D has been devoted to the production and development of functional products, such as anti-fatigue fabrics that can be used in outdoor sports underwear, knee pads, socks, and bedding products. Recently, they have been also developing a sports glove that exercises muscles while being worn.

The trade friction between China and the United States was on when Liang received an interview. She was very concerned about the mutual communication between the two countries, especially the intellectual property stressed by the United States. "The current trade barrier, in addition to the trade deficit, is

**Figure 6.9** Patents held by Liang company

intellectual property." Taking the textile industry as an example, she said that 70% of the world's textile products are made in China. The United States, which naturally senses the threat, badly wants to protect intellectual property rights. As a result, Chinese suppliers will experience more trade friction.

In 2017, Harvest suffered a storm in the US market. At that time, a new fabric product was selling so great that more than 90% of Amazon's related products were made of it. Seeing made-in-China everywhere, local companies sued Harvest's American sellers for infringement. According to American law, if it really constitutes infringement, the American seller will be doomed. The seller was panicking until Harvest provided the invention patent certificate. The lawsuit didn't go through. "In present international trade, patents are shields. Without it, products will probably not be sold abroad in the future," concluded Liang.

In conclusion, fine products should meet two requirements: one is to meet the needs of buyers in the Internet era, and the other is to lead the industry trends. At present, global buyers have become pickier, valuing product experience and naturally setting higher requirements for Chinese suppliers. In this respect, Liang, who has been in product R & D and design for 17 years, relates the most. She said that the Internet is not a battlefield where low-end products compete on price, but a platform where innovative elements participate in interactions and seek to quickly change and create new values. If Chinese suppliers still linger on made-in-China for foreign trade, they will easily be trapped in a difficult price war while suffering more challenges in international trade friction. Only by turning made-in-China into created-in-China with importance attached to the intellectual property rights of products can enterprises go far with heads held high.

*   *   *

## Fine service

Li Pengsen, born in 1991, looks delicate with her short hair. Despite her young age, she is capable. In just four years, her company has grown from two employees to 30 with an annual export volume of RMB 100 million. She is a rising star in foreign trade circles.

Li's hometown of Anping, in Hebei Province, is a famous at home and abroad for silk fishing nets. Most of the local businesses are family businesses and the overall economic development is relatively good. Many are content with things as they are. Li was not. She graduated from the Business English Department of the Hebei Institute of Foreign Languages a year in advance. After employment in Anping for some time, she decided to go to Shijiazhuang to start her own business.

However, the company's business was flat in 2014 and 2015. Ambitious, Li was eager to make a change. She began to learn everywhere, summarizing her learning and practical experience in writing and implementing it one by one. Since then, the company has witnessed a rapid development. In 2017, the export volume surged from US$6 million to US$13 million.

Li is diligent. As long as there is no business trip, she often arrives at the company in advance at 7 A.M. and composes her "foreign trade book" quietly at the computer. Hundreds of thousands of Chinese characters and English words have been written by now, including courses such as "Foreign trade from 0 to 1 to N" to help novices grow in stages, and "Three steps of small and micro enterprise management" to help business owners transform. The core of these courses is to provide high-quality services for buyers.

Fine service is a new trend among younger buyers. After fragmented orders and fragmented small orders on the Alibaba international station, higher requirements are put forward for the seller's service, which is a compulsory course for Chinese suppliers to take.

### More accurate display of products

Fine service is first reflected in the ability of information display. Suppliers can show themselves more accurately and professionally, provide high-quality commodity information and shop displays, and improve the matching degree of buyers' inquiries.

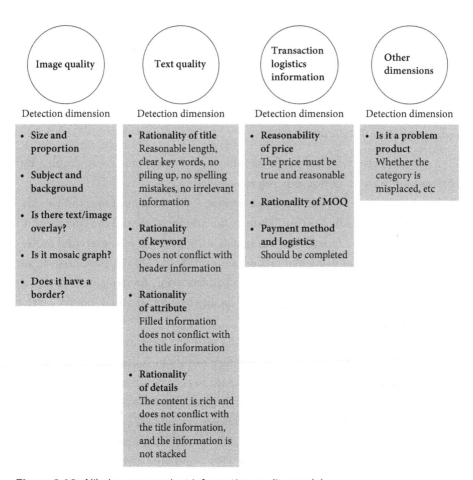

**Figure 6.10** Alibaba.com product information quality model

The presentation will also be more approachable to the perspective of young buyers and more diversified. In addition to the traditional text and image display, interactive experience, multimedia, short video are all new display forms. The application of VR technology in foreign trade transactions gives rise to VR inspection of plants, and customers can see them at home. Live broadcast online is another new way of information display, which connects online and offline uses.

In September 2017, Li performed extraordinarily on the global promotion of 920 Purchase Festival created by the Alibaba international station with a 10-day turnover of US $420,000. One of the reasons is the more diversified, precise, and professional display methods adopted for the three main products. Each product was equipped with short bilingual explanatory texts and videos. In the future, she plans to learn from Tmall stores to optimize the information display from the perspective of data, details, comparison, customer feedback, etc. So, the buyer is more willing to place an order, thus the workload of a salesman is reduced and there is more energy for customer service and focus on customer development and the product itself.

### More professional communication

Fine service is also reflected in the fact that both the response to an inquiry and communication with customers are professional.

Li used to work as a salesman. She divided the communications and negotiations with customers into the initial stage, the middle stage, and the later stage. In each stage, she summarized how to negotiate with the buyer efficiently and professionally step by step and taught it to the sales team. At the 920 Purchase Festival, she prepared 10 kinds of response strategies in advance only for price negotiation, so that sales staff could provide quick, high-quality, and professional inquiry service in the shortest time.

When communicating with a buyer, Li also has a set of standard processes to present the company's image. The primary display includes basic information, including the company's website, brand, address, contact person, principal business, and supplier scale; the intermediate display includes the introduction of procurement, sales season, procurement season, quotations, sales channels, etc. In different links, the salesperson switches different topics to meet the information needs of the buyer in time, therefore also improving the service quality at communication.

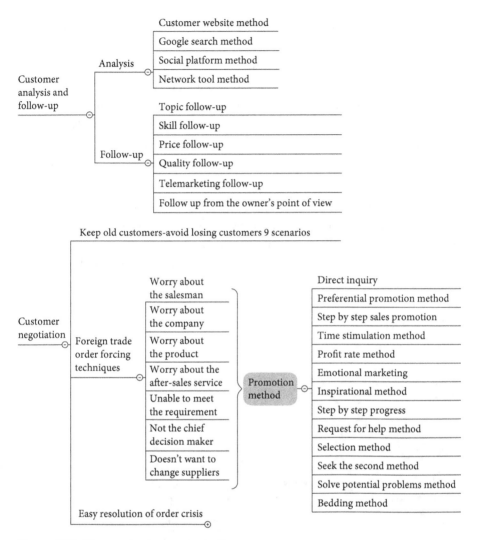

**Figure 6.11** Fine service in communication

## *Provide communication service with deterministic business opportunity*

Fine service involves a deterministic ability to communicate business opportunities and give buyers a better experience with a timely inquiry response.

Many overseas buyers have complained about the weak sense of time among Chinese. The promise of a phone call in 10 minutes is often not kept when over 10 minutes has passed. In terms of providing communication service with a deterministic business opportunity, Li would confirm with the other party a very predetermined time point, such as in 12 minutes or 27 minutes, and contact them as promised.

Among the key nodes of fine service, one criterion is to ensure that the communication service is made available within one hour. During the 920 Purchase Festival, Li's team operated 24 hours, easily ensuring communication service within one hour with a high response rate. Usually, employees get off work at 6:00 p.m., but within three hours from 6:00 p.m. to 9:00 p.m., the salesman must also reply to the buyer's inquiry within one hour. After work, the average reply time of each email is also within one-three minutes. Li herself stays online 24/7. When a salesman contacts her for an emergency, she can provide solutions in time, no matter how late.

Li herself has a clear idea that buyers' wireless transactions have increased significantly on the Alibaba international station. This makes order generation different from the past. It doesn't necessarily happen during working hours. During a meal, an inquiry may happen. After the number of daily active users increases, the new requirement for fine service is to stay sharp at communication with customers.

**Figure 6.12** Sales team of Li Pengsen's company

## *Visualization of production and supply capacity*

Fine service also extends to production and supply capacity, which requires that the key node data of production scheduling be visualized to buyers, so that they are posted about the progress of the order at any time.

This requires enterprises to fully grasp and ensure the production schedule of products. Li's company has a production scheduling department, which makes a production progress display board to have the salesperson understand the production progress at any time. Unlike many companies that passively respond to production progress only when the buyer asks, she chooses to take the initiative. A fixed time is set every week to inform the buyer of the production progress and regularly videos of the production process are made to send to the buyer. In this way, a seller naturally does not have to worry about the delivery time. "This is a process from push to follow, so that customers get used to us and trust in us," said Li.

## *Deterministic ability to ensure performance*

Performance guarantee is an indispensable link of fine service, which mainly refers to the implementation of a merchant according to the order requirements, so as to improve the buyer's experience and satisfaction.

First of all, the ability to ensure performance is to ensure that products meet the needs of the buyer, such as no incorrect deliveries. During the 920 Purchase Festival, the delivery volume of Li's company increased sharply, sometimes as many as hundreds or even thousands of pieces a day, resulting in a relatively high delivery error rate for the salespeople. To improve the buyer's shopping experience, Li made adjustment on the process in a timely manner, requiring salespeople and the production scheduling department to check and sign three times. Respectively, they were once after the order was placed, once after the bulk sample came out, and once after the bulk was completed. The delivery error rate was reduced to 20%. This process was subsequently perfected by the company. At the new trade festival in March 2018, the delivery error rate dropped to only 1%.

The ability to ensure performance is also reflected in the ability to for the seller and overseas customers to get in contact at any time. The competition in foreign trade industry is fierce, the pressure great, and salesmen often jump ships. Li adds a customer service email to every deal closed with her own contact information

**Figure 6.13** Basic daily workflow sheet of Li's salespeople

assuring the other party that her phone is reachable 24 hours a day. This gives the buyer a sense of being valued while making sure there is someone to solve the problems for customer if a salesman leaves.

### *Transform business thinking and cultivate modern business consciousness*

Li's awareness of the importance of service was raised when she met a Chinese American with a very large business in Hong Kong before her own entrepreneurship.

At that time, Li, a quick learner, asked him for the secret of success in foreign trade. The Chinese American didn't teach directly but pointed out a phenomenon that when loading cargos, the mainland Chinese businessmen never thought about the inconvenience of the other party's unloading. In mainland China, forklift trucks can load over two tons of goods while foreign ports are equipped with small forklifts able to load one ton of goods. It is difficult for workers to unload goods from China every time. "In the end, the dissatisfaction would go to the seller, who for this detail would lose future deals. Isn't that sad?" The Chinese American told Li that there are two keys to doing well in foreign trade. One is to understand how foreigners think, and the other is to pay attention to their purchasing habits. Li said that she was enlightened at once, realizing that the details of the service determine success or failure.

In 2015, Li started the foreign trade training for a factory consortium in Anping. In the first session, over 40 people signed up. Later, the number continued to increase. The venue was changed from 60 square meters to 200 and to 1,000 now. Having contacted a large number of front-line foreign trade personnel, Li found that many foreign trade companies failed to provide fine service to overseas buyers because the Chinese thinking patterns failed to understand international think patterns. Many who never really went abroad naturally would not understand how buyers think. For example, when many business owners instruct sales staff to negotiate prices, they always say, "We can't go any lower, otherwise there is no profit." This is the typical Chinese thinking. Overseas customers would assume that an unprofitable product's quality must be in question.

Li believes that to provide fine service, Chinese buyers must first change their business thinking, then have a modern business sense, build up a business style, then help customers solve problems they can't, and finally let them purchase care-free.

From being a rookie in the foreign trade industry to now, Li also encountered all kinds of confusion along the way. Especially in 2015, when the company had no management system, she took a passive attitude towards work. When she rendered the finest service she could at every single order, the company started to improve. Finally, in 2017, she achieved the goal of the export volume exceeding RMB 100 million.

Fine service has four dimensions: more accurate and professional self-display, the ability to communicate business opportunities with certainty, the ability to gradually realize the visual presentation of key node data of production scheduling to buyers in production and supply, and the ability to ensure the performance of the contract with certainty.

After more new elements, such as short video, live broadcasts, and VR enter foreign trade, rules are constantly changing. In the past, the traffic flow was the most important in online foreign trade. When the traffic came, a buyer could search for the corresponding goods. As e-commerce platform information became more transparent, traffic no longer is the most important. Chinese suppliers should adjust their thinking in time to provide buyers with high-quality service. According to the latest survey released by the Alibaba international station, future cross-border e-commerce trade is more than the display of texts and pictures, but interactive experience. By then, only those who provide fine services can take the lead in the new tide of change.

# EPILOGUE

One and a half centuries ago, Charles Dickens commented on Great Britain after the Industrial Revolution that it was the best of times, it was the worst of times. In the 21st century, the rise of Internet technology not only connects a world population of over seven billion into a community of common destiny, but also creates infinite new possibilities. As Klaus Schwab, founder and executive chairman of the world economic forum, put it in the Fourth Industrial Revolution, the fourth industrial revolution based on digital technology is coming. A series of open innovation will have China become a trendsetter of a new wave of economic activities and technological advancements.

In the best of times, future Chinese foreign trade enterprises should take the initiative to become fine businesses, representing the most pioneering power of global suppliers.

In the best of times, future Chinese foreign trade enterprises should take the initiative to provide fine products and demonstrate their responsibility towards global buyers.

In the best of times, future Chinese foreign trade enterprises should take the initiative to provide fine services to spread China's excellent business model and civilization concept.

I believe the efforts of numerous foreign trade enterprises will lead to the great change from made-in-China to China-made.

# About the Authors

LI XINXIN, Ph.D. in finance, Shanghai Jiaotong University, is the author of *Alibaba B+ Era: Empowering SMEs*. He has led over ten projects of Shanghai municipal government, such as Research on promoting comprehensive financial supervision system in Shanghai pilot Free Trade Zone, Study on linkage and risk prevention between financial innovation and the construction of Shanghai international financial center, Research on exploring new mode of industrial and financial cooperation and promoting financial innovation to serve real economy, launched by Shanghai Economy and Information Committee, and participated in 20 research topics, like the characteristics of Shanghai service industry development and trend analysis under the new normal launched by Shanghai development and Reform Commission. He has many publications on academic journals such as *Financial Research*. His focuses on the development of Internet and e-commerce while participate in the research on the bottleneck of cross border e-commerce in Shanghai launched by Shanghai Municipal Decision Advisory Committee. He is also invited to the third China (Shanghai) e-commerce development forum.

PENG XIAOLING graduated from Fudan University in 2007 with a master's degree in ancient Chinese literature. She has 11 years of working experience in mainstream media and now works in a well-known financial media as a news reporter in the fields of current politics, economy, people's livelihood, etc. She has been awarded with the Shanghai News Award and the Gold Medal of Shanghai Women's News.